APPLY THE LAWS IN THIS
SERIES AND EXPERIENCE

TRANSFIGURATION

Sister Thedra

Volume VII

Copyright © 2021 by Halls of Light, LLC

All rights reserved. This book or any portion thereof may not be reproduced or used in any manner whatsoever without the express written permission of the publisher except for the use of brief quotations in a book review.

ISBN: 978-1-7373071-1-2

TRANSFIGURATION

A complete change of form or appearance into a more beautiful or spiritual state. "in this light the junk undergoes a transfiguration; it shines"

The transfiguration is a sign that Jesus was to fulfill the Law and the prophets. It also assured James, Peter, and John the Jesus was indeed the Messiah.

In Christian teachings, the Transfiguration is a pivotal moment, and the setting on the mountain is presented as the point where human nature meets God: the meeting place for the temporal and the eternal, with Jesus himself as the connecting point, acting as the bridge between heaven and earth.

To the Reader

Please read and review "Divine Explanations" on page 234 for questions and definitions of terms.

This book is only a portion of the teachings and prophecies that have been given by Sananda (Jesus Christ), Sanat Kumara, and others of the higher realms, and Recorded by Sister Thedra.

Dedication

These volumes, entitled TRANSFIGURATION are dedicated to Sheryl McCartney and Kamalakar Durgapu, without whose invaluable assistance this work would not have been possible.

Contents

SORAN'S BLESSING 1

THOU ART OF THE 'FIRST BORN' 47

SHE - THE LIONESS 93

THE FIRST GENERATION 155

STRENGTH 195

Mission Statement 227

Sananda's Appearance 228

About the Late Sister Thedra 229

Divine Explanations 234

Other Books by TNT Publishing 245

Esu Jesus Sananda

This reproduction is from an actual photograph taken on June 1st, 1961, in Chichen Itza, Yucatan, by one of thirty archaeologists working in the area at the time. Sananda appeared in visible, tangible body and permitted His photograph to be taken.

SORAN'S BLESSING

Soran Speaking -- Mortals there be and mortals be as mortals. Sons of God there Be - and Sons of God shall ever Be ---

While Mortals are wont to know themself as Sons of God they deny the fortune of the Sons of God - that which is the inheritance of the Sons of God -- For they live within the mortal self - the mortal realm wherein they are but the sorry part of the Whole -- I say - they know not the fullness of their inheritance -- Their Sonship awaits their acceptance -- So be it that they shall come into it at the age of maturity.-

I say they shall come into their Sonship at the age of maturity - So be it that I Know – for I Am One of the Council and I Am free from bondage -- For I have never taken upon Mineself the <u>pore (physical body)</u> -- I am not of Earth born -- Never was I born of flesh -- So be it - I Am One of the Eloheim - and I speak as such -- So be it - I add Mine Blessing unto that which hast so generously been bestowed upon thee ---

I Am Come that ye be blest --

So let it be --

I AM Soran

Recorded by Sister Thedra of the Emerald Cross

The Time is Now

Wast it not said that there shall be great stress amongst the people of the Earth? -- And is it not so?

I say unto thee - the time swiftly approaches when there shall be great and profuse plundering - and great shall be the fear of the people They shall run about hither and yon seeking refuge - and there shall be no place to hide -- I say unto thee: These shall be the ones which have looked into the places wherein they are wont to go - for the poor part of wisdom -- They have been taught that they are the greatest of all generations - of all people - that their way is better than all other -- Yet it shall not suffice them - for they shall be caught up <u>short</u>-- They shall run riot! -- They shall slay their brothers - sisters - parents - children -- Their own shall they slay - yea - even themselves shall they slay!

I speak unto thee - that ye be prepared for the time which is at hand. Yea I say unto thee - the "Time shall try men's souls" - They shall go mad - and they shall cry out in their torment - knowing not that which torments them ---

While I say unto them: "Seek not the glory of men" -- Seek not the fortune of men -- I say unto them seek ye the Light - and It shall not be hidden ---

I say - rest ye assured -- Ye shall find no abiding place in the WORLD OF MEN -- Ye shall find Peace within the Law, the Light, The Peace of which I speak is not of men - it is of the SPIRIT - it is NOT of men! ---

Seek ye Peace - and know ye that the Peace of which I speak is of SPIRIT -- Be ye as ones which comprehend these Mine Words -- And let no fear be within thee - for I AM thine Shield and thine Buckler-- Wait upon Me and I shall lead thee from the dangers which beset the wayward - - And the hazard of men shall not touch thee ---

So be it and Selah ---

I AM Sananda

Recorded by Sister Thedra of the Emerald Cross

The Way of The Transgressor is Hard

Bor Speaking -- Wherein is it said that the Way of the transgressor is hard? -- Is it not So? ---

Thou shall see that which is their lot-- It is given unto Me to SEE and KNOW -- While they know not that which they fortune unto themself - they shall learn well their lesson - for this is their part - to learn! ---

Wherein is it said - the traitors are the saddest of the lot? So be it - And is it not obvious that the traitors are the ones which have not heeded the law that they have been given? So be it that they shall arise up against the Servants of God - and they shall mount their self-styled thrones - and deny the Power of the Almighty - the "ALL" "The Alpha The Omega" -- And they shall declare themself the Knowing ones. And for this shall they find themselves cut off! -- For they which doth deny "The Father" shall be as ones which do betray themself -- I tell thee - it is a pitiful fortune which they fortune unto themself -- So be it and Selah ---

Be ye no part of them -- Ask no favors of them-- Accept none - and give none -- Be ye as ones prepared for a New Part -- So be it - it shall profit thee ---

I AM

Bor

Recorded by Sister Thedra of the Emerald Cross

Come Let Us Rejoice!

Beloved Ones -- It is come when ye shall behold the Glory of the Lord. Ye shall have thine eyes opened unto the GLORY of THE LORD - and ye shall be glad ---

While thou hast NOT as yet beheld the fullness of HIS GLORY - thou shall come to SEE and KNOW the JOY of SEEING! ---

I say unto thee: "SEE THE GLORY OF THE LORD" and rejoice for thine SIGHT -- So be it -- I come that ye might be made to SEE -- So let it BE --

I AM Sananda

COME

And rejoice with Me --

Let us Sing the Glad Anthem together

So shall it Ring Out

COME - Let Us Rejoice!

Recorded by Sister Thedra of the Emerald Cross

There are Ones Which Sit in High Places & Call Themself 'wise'

Beloved of Mine Being -- Be ye blest of Mine Presence - and let it be recorded for them which know not - that there A<u>r</u>e ones which sit in high places - and call themself wise - which are instruments of the sinister forces -- There are those which sit in high places which are of the Mighty Council -- These s<u>ee</u> and k<u>now</u> that which goes on - and they are neither of a mind to assist them - nor bring them out of bondage. Yet these which <u>are</u> "Wise" are as the Silent Ones -- They deliver not great recitations and flowery speeches - that they might hold them spell-bound - that they might be called "Masters" or Wise Ones -- They <u>Care</u> <u>Not</u> for their fine titles - their puny degrees -- They have reached out a 'Silent hand' that the oppressed be delivered out ---

I say <u>aggression</u> shall end - and the aggressor shall be put to WOE which he shall bring upon himself -- He shall be brot low - and he shall no longer hold bound a people - a nation -- He shall be put to the test - and find himself wanting. So be it that I shall speak again of the two - the aggressors - and the oppressed ---

So be it - it shall be of Great Light - yet it shall not be that which they are wont to hear ---

Which is better - that which I SAY - or that which the oppressor sayeth? ---

So be it - I AM

Sananda

Recorded by Sister Thedra of the Emerald Cross

This Supersedes Faith

Sori Sori -- Be ye blest this day - and let it be understood that thou art not alone -- I say unto thee - thou ART NOT ALONE for I am close unto thee-- I Am with thee - and it is given unto thee to be weary of thine body / weary of feet --

And it is given unto Me to Know - for I see thee as ones weary of body -- Yet thine heart shall rejoice - for ye shall be made to leap for joy -- And thine bodies shall have no power over thee, For I say flesh is weak - and Spirit is Strong!

Spirit is not bound by flesh -- And it is for this that I say unto thee: Spirit is limitless/ boundless - and hast no limitations -- So be it that I know thee - and that which ye shall do ---

I say unto thee - hold ye steadfast and watch-- See that which I shall do - for I shall do a Mighty Work - and Ye shall be part of Mine Work, Part of the Great and Grand Plan ---

So be it - I Come that ye might know as I Know ---

I AM - Sananda

Recorded by Sister Thedra of the Emerald Cross

The Living Sacrifice

Sanat Kumara Speaking -- Beloved Ones - thou hast placed thineself upon The Altar of THE MOST HIGH LIVING GOD - that He might Glorify Himself in thee - thru thee -- So let it be ---

I AM COME that it BE -- For this do I lend unto thee Mine hand - that ye might be lifted up -- So be it that I have revealed Mineself unto thee as the "Most Worthy Grand Master" of the Inner Temple -- I AM that - and More - for I AM that which ye know not! Neither do any other know Me for that which I AM -- I AM the One which hast held the Earth for this day-- I have brot Her thru many Crises - as an ailing child-- I have watched Her and Her fortune - that She might not perish For Great is Her Part within this day--

She shall undergo great strain and stress -- Yet I say that a people is responsible for Her stress -- Yet the pain which She bears is obvious unto them which have eyes to see - and a mind to learn -- She reels and rocks as one given unto drunkenness -- And She gives forth Great pain and convulsions - for the reason that She hast taken upon Herself the suffering of mankind -- She hast been the Asylum of the laggards. And few know wherein She hast given of Herself, for long have they come and gone - leaving behind them the debris which they have created, caring n<u>o</u>t the results thereof. They refuse their own responsibility for such filth - such suffering - such a creation - as they have brot about.

While I say unto them - Clean it Up!! - They hear not - they are as ones which have not accepted their own responsibility -- <u>Now</u> it is come when they shall be removed into yet another place - and they shall learn W<u>ell</u> their lessons.

For it is come when there shall be a Great On-rush of Spirit - and they (the laggards) shall not endure the Light thereof -- They shall perish-- And then they shall be given a place liken unto their own kind and it shall be a n<u>ew</u> p<u>lace</u> wherein they shall be strengthened and brot to accountability---

Them which are not capable of these things which shall be the fortune of the laggards - shall be cast out - even as the chaff -- These shall be no more seen upon the Earth - neither within the Realms of Light - for they shall be NO MORE -- These shall be cast out and BE NO MORE! ---

It behooves Me to give unto thee this Word --

And for this hast thou accepted it - that it be given unto them which lament the fortune of these which are not capable of "Eternal Life" - There are ones which deny this Mine Word ---

Yet I ask them to examine the records - which are wont to be complete - which are <u>far</u> from complete - for they have d<u>elet</u>ed and scrapt much of the record which hast been given unto them -- Yet it is within the same as they have - that "these shall be Cast into O<u>ut</u>er D<u>arkness</u>"-- When they Know the meaning thereof - they shall understand that which shall be done this day -- So be it I have touched upon this subject and it is for the Good of All mankind - that I give it unto thee at this time -- So give it unto <u>Them</u> as I give it unto thee -- Be ye blest of Me and by Me - for I AM -

Sanat Kumara

Recorded by Sister Thedra of the Emerald Cross

They Have Their Hands in the Till

Beloved Ones -- This day I would say unto thee - there is Great turmoil within the world about thee -- They have their hands within the till - and their feet are as lead -- They go not forth to meet the new day - rejoicing -- They seek means of escape - thru - and by means which would be unto them their undoing -- I say they are wont to escape that which they have fortuned unto themself ---

While they know not the time of their <u>planting</u> - I say the seeds have been planted -- Now they are harvesting that which they have sown -- Yet this day I tell thee the seeds for the next harvest is being planted now -- And the season shall be short - and the harvest heavy -- The thistles and brambles shall torment them - and these they shall separate from the wheat - which shall be a long and painful task -- I say they shall harvest that which they have sown -- And they shall bear the burden thereof -- Therefore it behooves them to put within the soil perfect seed- which shall profit them ---

Weep not for them -- for they shall take their own responsibility - and thereby they shall come unto the "Age of Responsibility" and profit thereby -- Let it be said that their inheritance awaits them - when they have reached the Age of Responsibility ---

So be it that they shall be responsible for all their actions, their words - their deeds - for no man shall take from them the right to learn their lessons - and learn they shall -- So let it profit them ---

I Am come that it be well with them -that they learn - that they might go where I go --

So Be It - I AM

The Lord thy God

Sananda

Recorded by Sister Thedra of the Emerald Cross

The Zealots

While it is yet time - let it be said that there are many which ask of thee that they learn of Me -- Yet they ask of others that they learn of th<u>e</u>m - And wherein have they been edified? -- I say they are seeking within the realm of man- that they might reconcile their own beliefs -- So be it that I Am come that they have Light -- Yet they run hither and yon asking of men -- And they are the ones which have not the patience - neither the strength of Spirit to wait upon Me - the Lord thy God --

And I say unto thee - they ask of Me - they ask of men -- They then <u>coin</u> their own opinion from the many facets which they find - that differ so greatly -- Then they find themself at differences with ALL that they have questioned -- This is the pity of it -- They seek that which they <u>want</u> to find - and they are not prone to wait for the Greater Part -- They ask many questions concerning man - and his goings and comings - even their own - while they are not wont to ask of his origin or destination -- They but see the material sign posts that he has been this way - passed this way -- Let them <u>be</u> - for the zealot shall find that he too - shall be as one come alive! ----

So be it - I have answered thee ---

I AM Sananda

Recorded by Sister Thedra of the Emerald Cross

The Times at Hand

Beloved of Mine Being -- Bear ye in mind that there are none so sad as the ones which betray themself -- See that which THEY do - and be ye no part of their undoing -- See that which they DO! - and see that which they fortune unto themself -- Cry not for them-- Yet ye shall point the way - that they might know -- Yet when they turn from thee - and spit upon the hand which thou hast proffered unto them - let them be -- Give not the other - for they shall learn their lesson -- They shall give of themself in <u>Holy</u> surrender before it is finished --

They shall bow in Holy re<u>verenc</u>e before the ones which have held out a hand-- They shall cry out for M<u>erc</u>y - and ask for the hand which they have spat upon -- I say they shall be as ones crying out - and they shall be heard -- Yet they shall learn the bitter lesson - that "None are so sad as the one which betrays himself" -- So be it ye shall set before them the example -- Hold ye the Light - Stand steadfast -- Move not to the right nor to the left - and give no quarter -- For I say unto thee - the law is exacting -- Make ye no compromise with the forces of darkness -- And know ye that these are the days spoken of long ago - foretold within thine "Word" which is accredited unto the "Holy Writ" -- So be it sufficient that I say "This is the day for which thou hast waited - when the HOLY WRIT shall be fulfilled ---

So be it - I have spoken of The Times At Hand--

So Be It - I AM

The Lord thy God -

Recorded by Sister Thedra of the Emerald Cross

Creative Words & The Responsibility

Beloved Ones -- Behold the po_wer_ of the Word - and k_no_w it brings forth that which is made manifest within the realm of creation -- And be ye as ones blest to be the gi_ver_ and ta_ker_ -- And let not thine own words trip thee up -- For I say unto thee - ye live by the Word -- That which hast gone out of Mine mouth sh_all_ bless thee - and that which goes out of thine mouth sho_uld_ bless thee -- I say unto thee: "Bless thine self as ye would that I bless thee" --Yet it is given unto Me to see thee as ones forgetful of the power of the Spoken Word --

Ye fail to remember the power within the S_poke_n W_or_d-- It is said: "Let no word defile thine lips" -- NO word of hatred shall pass from thine lips -- And be ye not cast down - for the sake of the unknowing ones -- Hold high the "Torch of Freedom"-- Yet I say unto thee - <u>Free</u> thine own self from thine legiron -- Bind not thineself by the spoken word -- And bless thineself by the word which ye shall have made manifest - in thine world of manifestation -- I say - "Behold the Power of the WORD" -- See it manifest before thee -- Let it be thine freedom from bondage -- Forge not thine legirons -- So be it I speak for thine own sake --

Let it profit thee ---

I AM thine Lord God

Sananda

Recorded by Sister Thedra of the Emerald Cross

Hold Ye the Lamp High

Sori Sori - Hold ye the lamp high - that others might see the Light and be guided thereby -- Hasten ye to do the will of the Father - the Father which hast sent thee forth ---

Hold high the banner of freedom -- Let not thine lips betray thee -- Be ye as ones which take up the banner of freedom -- Let each be his own carter - his own porter -- Forch (force) not upon another that which is thine part -- Pity him not when he refuses that which hast been proffered him - for he shall learn well his lessons - and for this shall he profit ---

Let it be said that there are many which would misuse thee - and give unto thee the bitter dregs of their own cup -- Yet ye shall not partake of their cup - for they shall drink of their own bitters - that which they have fortuned unto themself ---

While it is given unto them to be walking within the shadows of many strange gods - they seek in far places for surcease from their pain - their misery -- Yet I say unto them - "Behold Me the Lord thy God - and hear ye that which I say unto thee"! Behold the Power of the Word and be ye glad -- For I say unto thee - "Come - follow ye Me - that ye might go where I go" -- So be it - I Am come to deliver thee up -- I say: Come! - Come unto Me and be made whole -- Come unto Me and be ye MADE WHOLE" ---

For this do I reveal Mineself this day --

Come and rejoice with Me --

I AM Sananda

Recorded by Sister Thedra of the Emerald Cross

Know Ye - The Way Has Been Made Clear

Behold Me the Lord thy God - "The Way" - "The Light"

I say unto thee Behold ME - and I shall lead thee out of bondage -- Seek ye first the Light - and the darkness shall disappear -- Know ye that the Way hast been made clear before thee - and it is given unto Me to be the Way Shower -- For t<u>his</u> have I said follow ye Me -- I Am

COME that ye might KNOW -- So be it that it is now come - when ye shall be as ones c<u>ome</u> a<u>live</u> -- And ye shall be as the ones which KNOW wherein thou art staid -- So be it that I AM thine STAY -- I seal thee within MINE LIGHT - for I AM the LIGHT -- I AM the ARMOR and the SHIELD ---

I AM thine Self- and at no time shall I forsake thee! ---

Yet - I say unto thee: - Know ye this - thou art the SONS of the MOST HIGH LIVING GOD - and thou art NOT alone -- So be it that thou art free to choose which way ye go -- Yet ye shall not fail thine Mission - neither betray thine trust -- It is clearly written that the ones which do turn back - are the saddest of the LOT!

So Be It - I AM the Lord thy God

Sananda

Recorded by Sister Thedra of the Emerald Cross

The Zealots
The Two Classes of "Them"

Soran Speaking -- It is Mine part to say unto thee this day - that there are ones which walk amongst thee - unknown/ unrecognized - and unsung/ uncrowned-- While they are of the Earth - they are bound by flesh- and walk as flesh - unrecognized by the unknowing ones - which are likewise bound in flesh / or the ones which have not awakened unto their true identity---

These which have come into thine midst as volunteers - that the flesh be lifted up - that the <u>Great</u> <u>Awakening</u> might be brot about - are the Shepherds - the Avatars - the Messengers - the Ambassadors/ the Royal Family -- And these are of 'Royal Lineage' -- They have not turned their face from their Source -- They are ones which have come for a <u>Divine</u> <u>Purpose</u> - and they <u>Know</u> that which they are about -- They are bound by their love for their fellow man - to give of themself that they be free - that they find their way home --

Yet here I speak unto the "Zealots"-- Let not thine zeal be unto thee thine own legiron/ the pitfall- For I say unto thee: "First prepare thineself for thine return - and put not thine foot into a hole" -- I say put not thine foot into a hole -- See ye clearly the way before thee - and walk ye with surety - that others might not stumble -- Walk ye upright that they might do likewise -- Be ye as one which has "Oil in thine lamp" - that they might see the Light. <u>Forch</u> not thine part upon them -- Take from them <u>not</u> their free will. Let them choose the way which they go -- Ask not that they follow thee. Let them hear that which the <u>Spirit</u> sayeth - and then they shall obey.

While it is given unto these - which have come as messengers/ as servants - they are the <u>hand</u>-<u>maidens</u> of the Lord - and they serve selflessly - and gladly-- So shall it ever be -- They are not prone to bragging to slothfulness -- Neither to bigotry or hypocrisy -- They are not wont to force their way into the house of another - that they subject him unto his favorite sayings - and unto his ideologies --

He is the humble servant - and serves where and when he is called of The Spirit He favors no man by his part - for he is no favorite of persons -- He is at ALL times fortuned the part which is necessary unto his Work - and he asks of no man favors -- He imparts only Truth and

Light -- So be it I have spoken unto thee of the Ones which are the Servants - and of the ones which know not - let them awaken! ---

I AM Soran

Recorded by Sister Thedra of the Emerald Cross

For the "Record"

This day let it be recorded - that they which follow after thee - might know that which I have said unto thee -- It is for this that I say: "Record that which I say unto thee" ---

Let it be understood that the Ones which I have appointed as MINE MOUTH - MINE VOICE - are as MINE OWN VOICE - MINE OWN MOUTH -- And at no time shall they set foot against One of Mine Appointed Servants- for great shall be their sorrow ---

Now let it be understood that I am not unmindful of Mine Servants Mine fore-sworn/ worthy Servants -- For this hast they been called - and appointed - for their worthiness -- Let not thine voice be raised against these which I appoint! ---

I am not unmindful of them!! I Am a Merciful One -- I KNOW what I Am about - and I am not asleep -- I Am alert unto their every need - and therein I shall be unto them sufficient - So be it I have spoken and I Am NOT finished ---

I AM Sananda

Recorded by Sister Thedra of the Emerald Cross

Hold Ye the Lamp

Sori Sori -- Hold ye the lamp high -- Hold high the Banner which I bring - which I give unto thee -- Hold ye steadfast unto the Light which I AM -- And KNOW ye that I AM the LORD THY GOD - COME THAT THERE BE LIGHT --- SO LET IT BE ---

Now ye shall be as ones prepared to give unto them as ye have received -- Ye shall KNOW the TRUE from the false -- And for this ye shall go forth as ones prepared -- Ye shall go forth declaring the TRUTH - and it shall be upon their shoulders - if they reject it -- So be it there are ones which shall raise up against thee - and they shall deny the "Word" and reject thee -- So be it they shall bear the responsibility for their own foolishness - and unknowing-- For I have said: "SEEK YE THE LIGHT" - yet they look unto men - and ask of their opinions and follow after strange and false gods -- They bow down before their altars - and worship them which have bound them fast -- So be it and Selah ---

I say they have not the Light -- So be it they shall first ASK of THE FATHER - the GIVER of LIFE / LIGHT -- and then they shall KNOW.

They are now bound by their opinions/ dogmas/ creeds and they are wont to seek Me out -- So be it I stand ready to assist them - when they turn from their dogmas - and creeds - and seek their freedom WITHIN ME -- So be it that I AM FREE -- I AM prepared to LEAD THEM WHERE I GO - So be it and Selah ---

I AM Sananda

Recorded by Sister Thedra of the Emerald Cross

Brotherhood / Benefactors Obedience - Ethic

Soran -- Beloved Ones -- It is Mine part to give unto thee this Word - and it shall be given unto them - as I give it unto thee -- It shall be given unto them which receive it - to have the Word before them - and they shall see that which hast been said -- It shall be unto them Mine testimony and Mine part - which is meant to prepare them for the days ahead -- Now let it be said - that there are MANY days ahead -- yet the time is not afar off - when they shall cry out in bewilderment -- And they shall not know which way to go -- They shall be glad for the help of the Brotherhood -- I say mock not thine <u>Benefactors</u> - for They are not the puny ones which KNOW NOT! ---

I say They ARE thy Benefactors - They are not wanting ---

I say: They ask of thee nought - except obedience unto the law set before thee - Yet ye shall not be divided against thineself -- Ye shall serve the Lord thy God with ALL thine STRENGTH - ALL thine MIND - ALL thine BEING!! -- And ye shall not make a mockery of thine speech -- Ye shall be as ones mindful of thine Words -- Let not thine lips belie thine BEING -- I say unto thee - be ye as the SERVANTS of the LIVING GOD - and serve HIM diligently - for thou art as ones ABIDING WITHIN HIS GRACE -- It is by <u>HIS</u> GRACE that thou ART -- So be ye mindful of HIM -- Let thine heart be glad - and thine lips shall be quick to sing HIS PRAISE -- Yet I say again - be ye not deceived - for thou art not wont to obey the law which HE gives unto thee ---

Deceive not thineself - give unto Him ALL the Praise - ALL the Glory - and feign not wisdom -- for wisdom is a gift of the Holy Spirit.

So be it I speak unto thee of things which are of the Spirit -- So be it I say unto thee: "HEAR YE THAT WHICH THE SPIRIT SAYETH".

So be it - it shall profit thee ---

I AM Soran

Recorded by Sister Thedra of the Emerald Cross

The Beginning - The End

The "ALL"

Mine Children -- I AM thine Father SOLEN AUM SOLEN -- I AM the Father Eternal - ever was - and ever shall BE -- While thou art Mine Children and ever shall ye be -- for I have given unto thee BEING -- Of Mine Self hast thou thine BEING -- Thou art not of the nether world Thou ART OF ME - and BY ME -- I have sent thee forth as the Part of ME - which I have called "Children"- <u>thrust</u> <u>forth</u> as thine hand is thrust out before thee -- So do I hold thee out - and I sustain thee of Mine Being - even as thine own hand is sustained by thine form - and thine own individual heartbeat and breath ---

I say unto thee - thou art "ETERNAL BEINGS" - and thou art sustained by Mine Pulse - Mine Breath - for without this - <u>thou</u> <u>wouldst</u> <u>not</u> <u>BE</u> ---

While thou hast not the mind to comprehend the fullness of Me - thou ART OF ME - born of ME art thou-- While thine Earthly form is but a <u>garment</u> - which thou dost wear but a time - it shall be cast aside as the substance which it is - and ye shall step forth into thine body of Light Substance - pure in its Substance-- For this Substance is that from which ALL THINGS are made -- The body of which I speak shall not bind thee-- It shall be unto thee that which I AM -- Therein ye shall know freedom - as thou hast not -- Thou shall be free to GO into ANY place - for thou shall be One with that place --

And ye shall have no need of time - neither space - for space is limited by time - and by the mind of men -- I say ye shall be free of time / space and matter - for matter shall no longer bind thee -- Ye shall be as One with ME -- Ye shall know thineself to BE ONE WITH ME - and ye shall be glad -- So be it I have spoken - and thou hast heard Me - for thou ART ONE in ME and OF ME! -- I AM the ALL -- I AM the Father - the Mother - the Beginning - the End - the ALL

Recorded by Sister Thedra of the Emerald Cross

Behold Thine Self
(Know Thine Self)

Behold in Me the Light Which I AM -- Behold in Me the Light which thou art - and know ye that I AM the Lord thy God --

For this I speak unto thee this day - "Behold Thineself - and Know ye that I AM - and Thou Art as one with ME" -- For this hast thou received Me -- Let it be known that I Am come that there be Light - that there BE LIGHT! ---

I Say: -I AM COME THAT THERE BE LIGHT - So let it BE --- For this have I given unto thee the power and the authority to speak for

Me -- Thou (Thedra) hast received Me unto thineself - and I have placed Mine hand upon thee - and pronounced thee Mine Own Messenger -- And I have commissioned thee to give unto "them" that which I say unto thee -- Yet thou shall keep for thineself that which is for thee -- For there are ones which would but defile themself - and be unto themself the traitor -- While they would but deny Mine Word - and spit upon thee - I say it is the better part of wisdom to withhold the part which is for thineself alone -- So be it ye shall share with "them" thine cup - when they are able to bear it -- For they are as infants - which cannot partake of strong drink---

I say - they are as yet liken unto the infant- they can not partake of the "Strong drink" -- They are as the weakling -- They drink of the bitter cup- and call it sweet -- Yet they fall by the ways - crying for surcease from their torment -- While I say unto them - pour out the wine of Great Strength - and I shall give unto thee WATER - more potent -- So be it I speak unto them which have not tasted of the Cup which I proffer them ---

I say unto them: DRINK OF MINE CUP - and it shall sweeten thine belly --

So be it I speak unto thee in parables - which thou canst understand. To them which have ears to hear - I say: "Hear ye that which I say" - and be ye as ones Prepared for Greater Things ---

I AM Sananda

Recorded by Sister Thedra of the Emerald Cross

The Mighty Council Which is Over All

Sons of God are WE -- WE are the ONES which comprise the Mighty Council which is OVER ALL - Which directs the Courts - the Plan - Which wast established in the beginning -- For from the beginning wast ALL things <u>Created</u> - by- and according unto the Law - the First Principle -- And according unto this Law hast the lands - the waters - and the fullness thereof come into being ---

Now I say unto thee: - There is a law governing ALL things - and according unto it do We of THIS MIGHTY COUNCIL move/ act -- And within this Council do We have the power and authority to do that which is beyond the power of the So-called Potentate / Priest / King / Judge or Prophet - of Earth -- <u>They</u> come under the law of the Earth -- Yet the Earth is under the Law of which I speak -- The laws of Earth are subject unto the Law of the "First Cause" - and it is Our Part to direct the people --

THE GREAT CAUSE hast no preference of a people -- They are many - and within the MANY are ones which have come into embodiment that "<u>that</u> <u>people</u>" be lifted up -- Such is Mine part -- Yet I come that ALL PEOPLES be lifted up -- While others have come - <u>I</u> <u>Am</u> the One Sent that <u>ALL</u> <u>PEOPLE</u> be lifted up - for I AM the SON which is of the FIRST BORN - and I AM HE which is the LORD GOD - over ALL -- And they which have come that "A People" be lifted up - come under the head of the MIGHTY COUNCIL of which I AM the HEAD---

So be it that I AM not bound by <u>any</u> <u>name</u> - creed - nor dogma -- I Am known as SANANDA - and I Am the One which hast revealed Mineself unto thee many years ago (in thine time) - or in thine manner of calculating time -- For in ages past - thou hast known Me as <u>Such</u> - and as such ye shall know Me -- No man shall deny Me Mine Name - for it is not within their power to deny Me Mine Inheritance - the Power which Mine Father hast given unto Me ---

Now for this do I give unto thee the power and the authority to speak for Me - for I shall give unto thee the Words to say -- I shall put Mine Words in thine mouth -- I shall make of thee a fearless and shining vessel - and it shall not be as tinkling brass- it shall be as one filled with Light and shine forth - that they which thirsteth might drink thereof -- I say I shall give unto thee of Mineself that ye be filled to overflowing And it shall be for this that the words shall pour forth from thine mouth as Mine --

I say the words which shall pour forth from thine mouth shall be <u>Mine</u> - and they shall Glorify Me - even as Mine Words Glorify Mine Father -- So be it that I come unto thee that they might KNOW of Me - and learn of Me -- So let it be - for as they prepare themself - so shall they receive -- And it is now come when I shall touch them - as is the way of the Lord -- I shall QUICKEN them - and they shall come to KNOW ME - even AS I AM -- So be it and Selah --

I AM THAT I AM -- Say unto them as I would say - I AND MINE FATHER ARE ONE -- And they too shall revile against thee -- Yet Know ye that I AM with thee -- I AM thine shield and thine buckler.

I AM Sananda

Recorded by Sister Thedra of the Emerald Cross

Those Who Do & Those Who Do Not Serve the Law of Justice

Beloved of Mine Being -- This day I would say unto thee-- Give of thineself that others have this Word -- Let it bless them that receive it - as it shall bless thee -- For this is it given - that it bless them -- And thou shall be blest of Me and by Me -- So let it be -- While it is now come that they shall weary of that which they have fortuned unto themself - and that which they are wont to perpetuate - and that which shall be unto them great sorrow -- I say they shall weary of that which they have fortuned unto themself ---

Yet they shall bear the responsibility of their own part -- They shall learn that they are not the ones which have made the law of Justice - neither have they been servants of the law of Justice -- They have served the forces of darkness - and they have not given of themself that there be Light within them ---

They have been as BIGOTS - filled with self-hatred - and with many opinions -- Yet they are not mindful of the Law which is set before them -- They are prone to forgetfulness -- They are not mindful of their part in the distress which covers the Earth - and they call themself "Innocent"---

I say they are not innocent -- They have been unto themself traitors! They have sold their birthright for a poor penny! ---

I say unto thee - pity are they -- They are poor in spirit - and they shall learn well their lessons -- For this shall they be prepared -- It is the LAW that they learn ---

So be it that ALL the LAW is given unto them - which is sufficient for their salvation - if they but abide thereby -- So be it I shall speak again of this-- Be ye as one prepared to receive it - that they might know that which I say - for I shall speak out against the <u>oppressors</u> and the BIGOTS ---

I shall declare the TRUTH openly - that they might <u>Know</u> that they are wanting - that they shall be responsible for their foolishness ---

So be it I shall speak unto thee at a later hour - - - Wait --

I AM Sananda

Recorded by Sister Thedra of the Emerald Cross

One

Give unto Me credit for Being that which I AM -- Give unto thineself credit for being ONE with ME -- And give unto the FATHER SOLEN AUM SOLEN - ALL the CREDIT - ALL the PRAISE - ALL the GLORY forever and forever - So let it BE -- For this do I speak unto thee <u>this</u> day --

I Am come that ye might KNOW THINE ONENESS - and that ye might KNOW that HE is the CAUSE of thine BEING - and that thou art not alone -- Thou art not separate from HIM - therefore thou art not separate from ME -- I AM the Lord thy God and THOU ART ONE WITH ME -- Too - I say:- Behold thineself in ME -- Behold thine SELF - And SEE ME ---

KNOW ye that thou ART ONE with ME -- Let it be said that I AM that I AM -

Sananda

Son of God -

The All

Beloved -- Wherein is it said that I AM THE ALL - the FATHER MOTHER SON - the BEGINNING - the END -- I create of Mineself - and I come not - neither do I go -- Yet I AM - the CAUSE of the coming forth and the going out-- I create and I cast off -- Yet I AM no less - for I AM the sum total. While Mine hand can not know the sum total of ME -<u>as</u> Mine hand - it is no less the hand -- The foot knows not the hand -- So be it that I AM the HEAD -- I AM that which is <u>ABOVE ALL</u> -- I command and Mine hand and foot moves in harmony - in rhythm and precision -- So shall it BE - for I AM that I AM ---

Be it ever SO - for I AM

Solen Aum Solen

Recorded by Sister Thedra of the Emerald Cross

HOW Do We Know?
The Difference Between the Thinkers & the Knowers

Beloved of Mine Being -- This day let it be recorded for them which are to follow thee - that they might see that which hast been said unto thee -- That they might KNOW that which hast been said -- And it shall profit them - for the records shall be KEPT - and they shall be as the HOLY WRIT -- The written records shall be the "WORD" by which they shall abide -- And they shall KEEP it pure and unadulterated -- It shall NOT BE CHANGED - ONE IOTA -- It shall maintain the POWER with which it is sent forth -- And it shall carry with it <u>that</u> power and purity -- It shall be unto them the Light which <u>they</u> seek -- They shall hold it SACRED - and be blest forevermore ---

I say - <u>woe</u> unto any one <u>whosoever</u> which doth adulterate the WORD - which is given herein - for it is given from out the Light - from out the LIGHT SUBSTANCE --And it is given in its simplicity and purity - with no pretense unto their long and complicated and "learned" sermons - doctrines/ creeds/ and dogmas --

I say: - Let not their creeds - dogmas and sermons bind thee or trip <u>thee</u> up -- For I Am come that ye have Light - and that ye know the TRUTH -- for I AM the LIGHT - the TRUTH and the WAY -- So be it that I shall lead thee out of bondage -- I say:- Follow ye ME - and be ye not concerned with their creeds and dogmas - for it but binds them - <u>hands</u> <u>and</u> <u>feet</u>! ---

So I say unto them which ask for Light - be ye <u>one</u> with it - and ask NO man's opinion of ME - for "they" know ME not!

They which <u>think</u> - <u>know</u> <u>not</u>!

They are the THINKERS!

I come that ye might KNOW ---

So let it be well with thee ---

I AM Sananda

Recorded by Sister Thedra of the Emerald Cross

Divine Law is unchanged

Beloved Ones -- These Mine Sons have been sent unto the children of Earth that they be lifted up -- For this do I now send them unto thee - that ye might <u>know</u> as they know -- For long hast thou - O Child of Earth - wandered in darkness -- Thy time hast been heavy upon thee -- Thine mind hast been as nought -- For thou hast "thought" - and to think is the beggardly part -- To think is the poor part -- I say - to KNOW is WISDOM -- Then ye shall walk with surety -- I say unto thee:- Behold the Light -- Seek ye the Light - and it shall come forth - that ye might be <u>one</u> with it ---

Hear ye that which the SONS OF GOD say unto thee -- I say unto thee fear not - for nought save Light shall protect thee -- Nought save darkness shall bewilder thee -- I say thou art bewildered children - thou knowest not which way - neither wherein - lies thine freedom -- I tell thee O children - heed ye Mine Word - "Seek ye Truth and Justice" - and know ye <u>Justice</u> -- Know that there <u>is</u> Justice --

Know ye the LAW and abide therein -- Do that which is required of thee - and turn neither to the left or the right -- Hold ye steadfast unto the LAW - for the LAW changes not -- I say unto thee - man does not change the LAW-- They are not capable of changing the LAW of which I speak -- I say unto thee - WATCH! LOOK! LISTEN! -- Hear that which I say unto thee - for I AM the Father which hast sent the Sons of God unto thee - that ye might know the LAW ---

So be it I AM

Solen Aum Solen

Recorded by Sister Thedra of the Emerald Cross

To the Ones Who Sanction Capital Punishinent

Soran Speaking -- Let this be given unto them which ask for Light -- Let them see that which I say unto thee -- Let it be known that they shall NOT make a mockery of the LAW -- It is of Great concern unto US of the Mighty Council - that they have gone so far as to defy the LAW---

It hast ever been so - yet not at any time have <u>they</u> been so brazen in their defiance ---

They have taken upon themself the part of <u>creator</u> and <u>destroyer</u>!

They have given unto themself credit for being JUDGE of all humanity - and <u>of the</u> <u>LAW</u> -- yet they obey not the first commandment given unto them ---

They know not <u>themself</u> - yet they set themself up as judge of their brethren -- While they take from him his rights - his "soul" deprived of its vehicle - which they are want to take from him - they are as ones which know not the results thereof ---

They know not that they unleash the Spirit which is bound upon the Earth by its (Earths) law - (and therein is the pity) - they are unaware that - that <u>Spirit</u> - Earth-bound as he is - is want to express itself thru another which knows not!

I say it is a vicious practice - and it shall stop! Yet it is within the power of man to stop it - for they have the <u>voice</u> -- The way is now made clear - that they stop their vicious practices -- Let it be said:- that <u>any</u> man whosoever which desires the life of another is GUILTY OF MURDER! ---

I say unto them - they stand as condemned before the law - for the law is just - and plays no favorites-- So be it they condemn themself - therefore shall they be found wanting ---

I Am come that they might have the part which is willed unto them of the Father - which hast given unto them life ---

I say unto them: Stop! Look! See! - and know that there is MORE there is MORE ---

Know thineself and be <u>ye</u> responsible for thine own acts/ thine words/ thine deeds/ and forgive thine self thine own offenses - and hold ye the Light that others might see and know that there is Light - that there is the WAY in which they might go - wherein they might find themself ---

So be it - I speak that it be so ---

I AM Soran -

Recorded by Sister Thedra of the Emerald Cross

Solen Aum Solen

Be ye as Mine hand and Mine foot - and do ye that which I give unto thee to do -- Let thine hand be swift to record this Mine Word - that they might know that which I say unto thee -- Let it be recorded thusly "Few there be which know Me as I AM"-- I AM the ONE which hast sent thee forth as part of Mineself - as Mine hand thrust forth -- I say - as Mine hand thrust forth - have I sent out Mine Children - as Mine own Self made flesh ---

I say - as Mine Own Self made flesh - I have sent forth Mine Children -- "SONS! Have I sent that they might Glorify Me in flesh -- Yet it is come when they which have slept the sleep of the <u>unknowing</u> shall awaken - and they shall return unto Me - as ones "Awake" - as ones justified - purified - and made WHOLE ---

So be it that I AM the Father Eternal -

Solen Aum Solen -

Recorded by Sister Thedra of the Emerald Cross

The Point of No Return
Order of Melchizedek

Herein is the Word of the Ones which have <u>guarded</u> and <u>guided</u> thee - which have given of themself in devotion and <u>service</u> unto the "Great Plan" -- Now it is said that they have defied the law - they have set themself up as the "Wise" -- They boast of <u>their</u> accomplishments - giving <u>no</u> <u>credit</u> to them of "Other Worlds" - <u>other</u> <u>realms</u> - for their

Being -- They think they are alone? ---- I say unto them: "YE ARE NOT ALONE"! -- And they have fortuned unto themself a sad fortune for they have made it necessary for US of the Mighty Council to take action!! ---

I say: We have taken action! -- Yet within THE LAW -- We have not transgressed the Law given unto US of the Order of Melchizedek - I too say - the Order of Melchizedek is the Brotherhood of Man - which know themself to BE ONE WITH THE FATHER which hast given unto US the LAW ---

WE have not transgressed this LAW - for We are aware of the consequence thereof -- The way of the transgressor is different from Our Way - Ours is of Light - theirs of darkness -- We Know - they THINK! - and know not -- While they have gone so far as to give unto themself credit for being WISE! ---

I say they have prepared for themself the "bitter cup" - so let them drink thereof -- It is clearly written - that they which are the traitors - shall be as ones removed from the Earth - and placed within a place wherein they may (or shall) torment each other until they weary of their lot - then - they shall first know that they are responsible for their own deeds -- Then they shall seek the Light - and IT shall NOT be denied them ---

T H I N K ye NOT that ye are alone! - For in Mine FATHER'S house are MANY Mansions ---

I say unto them: "I come that ye might go where I GO" -- Yet they seek the lesser part -- They give unto them the poor part - while they Know Not the fullness of the Plan -- I say - they have sold their inheritance for a poor penny -- So be it I come that there be Light - so let it be -- It shall be given unto them to go far afield - and they shall go to the point of NO RETURN! -- So be it I speak unto thee that they might KNOW that which I say -- Let them which have ears to hear - hear that which I say - it is for them that I speak out this day ---

I shall raise Mine Voice - and they which have ears shall hear - and KNOW that I have spoken TRUTH ---

So let it be - I AM the Lord thy God -

Sent that there be Light -

Recorded by Sister Thedra of the Emerald Cross

For This Have I Said: The Father and I are One

Beloved Ones -- This day it is given unto Me to speak unto thee - and it is for the good of ALL - it is for the benefit of ALL -- Yet there shall be ones which shall deny this Mine Word -- It is said that there are few which know Me as I AM - and there are few which seek the Light which I AM -- Yet they are as Ones which have little light -- They are as ones which have given unto Me credit for Being that which I AM - yet they know not the FULLNESS of ME - THAT WHICH I AM ---

While it is given unto them to limit Me - in their concept of ME - I say they have "little light"-- Yet it is now come when they shall be given even Greater -- For it is now come when they shall ask for Greater Light - Greater Comprehension - and a Greater Capacity for knowledge of ME -- While I say unto them "Know thine Self and ye shall Know

ALL MEN" -- And for this have I said: The Father and I ARE ONE -- So BE IT and Selah --

I AM Sananda

Recorded by Sister Thedra of the Emerald Cross

The Wanderer

1st letter
Responsibility

I Am He which is known as the Wanderer -- I Am He which tarried - and I Am He which was saddened for the waiting - yet wait I did -- Yea LONG I waited ---

While it wast given unto Me to wait - I <u>expected</u> the return of Mine Lord – N'ere <u>once</u> did I <u>doubt</u> His promise – N'ere did I give unto Him the bitter cup -- For I KNEW HIM -- and I kept Mine faith in Him and his Word unto Me ---

For <u>this</u> do I now say unto thee: I AM WITH HIM - within the place wherein He Is -- I give of Mineself that I might be as One with Him -- I give of Mineself that I might come unto thee - even as He ---

Let it be established for ALL TIME that He is the LORD GOD - sent of Our Father that the age of darkness might end ---

It hast been long - yet the Age of Light swiftly approaches -- Yet it is now established that <u>some</u> shall be removed - <u>knowing</u> <u>not</u> that it is come - for there are ones which are not capable of receiving the "Light"

These are the ones which shall be put into another place - wherein <u>ye</u> shall <u>not</u> go - for ye shall not be one of them -- It is said: that each shall be put into his own environment - and he shall <u>not</u> be as one <u>prepared</u> to enter into the place of "HIS" abode -- He shall not be the one to enter into the Holy of Holies - for his desire -- For this hast he been given the Law - that he apply it unto himself -- He hast been given the Law that he have ample time to work out his <u>own</u> Salvation ---

There are none which shall do it for him -- There are ones which are the <u>unknowing</u> <u>ones</u> which have taught the doctrine of "Vicarious Atonement" - yet it is an unjust doctrine - without foundation - for it is not lawful" ---

The Father is JUST -- The Father is merciful and patient in all things -- There is no inconsistency in the Law!! ---

THE LAW clearly states: "<u>Thou</u> <u>shalt</u> <u>Not</u> <u>Kill</u>"- now it is said that <u>The</u> <u>Father</u> sent His Son to die upon the CROSS! -- Nay! Nay! Mine blessed ones - Nay! Nay! -- It wast known - yet not the Plan of Our Father for He hast not provided such a diabolical law - that One atone for another-- Yet He hast made it possible that ALL men be responsible for themself!

That Is the Law -- ALL "men" shall come into the age of accountability - and be <u>self</u>-responsible - responsible for themself! ---

I say unto thee - <u>this</u> <u>is</u> <u>the</u> <u>law</u> -- No other man pays his price - or his <u>ransom</u> -- He hast NO SCAPE GOAT -- So be it - I too know the law - for long have I been the "'Wayfarer" upon the Earth - and for this have I learned the laws of Earth - and the "Greater Law" of which I speak - and of which I would they ALL learn ---

While the waiting is long and hard for them which await Him - I say it shall be the Great reward when He makes Himself Known unto thee ---

For n'ere again shall ye be satisfied with thine old part/ opinions/ loves/ and hatreds -- These shall depart from thee - and ye shall see them no more---

I say unto them which seek the Light: "Bear thine own cross with thanksgiving - mercy - love and understanding" -- Judge not thine fellow-man - by thine own stature -- Sit not in the seat of the scorner - Let thine own Light so shine that all might know that thou art the follower of Him which IS COME ---

I come that I might add Mine love and blessing unto His.

I Am - His devoted Brother - known as the "Wanderer" -- Be ye blest this day - and give ye the first of Mine letters unto them which ask for the Word -- So be it I shall speak again --

So be it I AM

Recorded by Sister Thedra of the Emerald Cross

2nd Letter - The Initiate

Beloved: I speak unto thee this day as the "Wanderer" and I say unto thee: Behold the hand of God - SEE IT MOVE - and KNOW ye that there is POWER in "THE WORD" - for IT shall be made manifest ---

Now ye shall give unto them this Word - and it shall profit them to see and to hear that which I say-- For it is given unto Me to know whereof I speak -- Now ye shall be Mine hand made manifest - for this Mine Word unto them -- It is for this that I give it unto thee - that they might know that which I Am about to say ---

For the first time I say unto thee - it is Mine part to be with the Lord God - The Host of Hosts -- I Am One of the Host - and I Am not of a mind to mislead thee -- When it was given unto Me to wander the Earth over - for MANY long centuries - waiting the return of the "MASTER" Mine Lord - I wast not unmindful of Him -- I KNEW that He should return - yet I knew not the hour - the day - nor the year -- Yet I say that the waiting wast <u>hard</u> AND FRUITFUL - for it brought Me great KNOWLEGE of Mine fellow-men - and of the Earth and the fullness of Her Joy and Sorrow -- Her mysteries were revealed unto Me -- Yet I needed no puny fruit or herb - to induce sleep OR wakefulness -- I needed little sleep - little did I rest - for I wast want to go unto Mine Lord ---

I worked mightily and diligently - that I prepare Mineself for to receive Him -- For this wast the fulfillment of Mine long waiting ---

I knew it would end in GREAT JOY - such as I had not known -- Yet it is not given unto Me to interpret such Joy unto thee in words of any language-- While it is something which each and every Initiate shall come to understand - and to know as I did - as I DO ---

I say unto thee - EACH AND EVERY INITIATE shall experience such JOY as I - when they behold HIM in all HIS GLORY -- So be it - it can not be put into words - for JOY is not of word - or for that matter it is not of flesh - for flesh hast not the STRENGTH OF CHARACTER or the NATURE to endure such as Spirit can reveal -- It is BEYOND All human comprehension ---

Now let it be recorded thusly:

THE INITIATE KNOWS of the JOY which He cannot convey unto the un-initiated - for he hast not as yet the mind to comprehend -- He knows not the JOY of the Initiate ---

While the Initiate walks silently - humbly - and gives heed unto the Law set before Him - the uninitiated rushes about babbling - and knows not that which he says -- He is boastful of his accomplishments - and he has not as yet learned the first lesson-- He is a braggart -- He goes his own willful way- asking of man favors - and of his opinion - seeking rewards of men -- So be it this is Mine Second Letter unto thee for them which hast a mind to learn of Me --

So be it I bless thee with Mine Presence and Mine Love --

I AM known as -

The Wanderer

Recorded by Sister Thedra of the Emerald Cross

The Infinite Hand

Beloved Ones -- Mine hand is not shortened - it is extended out into all the lands - into the waters of the seas - into the Cosmos - and all the Galaxies – "Infinity" is <u>Mine</u> - NOW - and ever shall be - for I AM the ALL - the Endless ---

I AM the first - the last - the <u>Beginning</u> and the <u>End</u> ---

For from ME all Eternal things hast come into manifestation -- And they shall return unto ME - for I expand Mineself that they might BE - I <u>recall</u> that which I send out -- I send out - I bring back -- I expand - and I bring into manifestation that which is made manifest -- I Am no less - no greater-for the manifestation is of ME - IT IS ME -- And when it hast served its purpose - I withdraw Mine thought - and it is no longer Mine instrument - Mine Power - for I withdraw the power which hast held the manifested form <u>in</u> <u>form</u> ---

There is a mold in thought - "thought form" - and that form is held until the manifest action is ready to be brought forth - as something dense - and seen by the material eyes of men -- It is the seen world - the material world of form - that man concerns himself with -- I say it is the material world which shall pass and be no more - while that which animates it shall <u>not</u> pass - for it is the Essence out of Which ALL manifestation is made manifest ---

Now let it be understood that the time is upon thee - that ye shall come to <u>know</u> the T R U T H which shall unbind thee - and it shall be a glad day -- So BE IT and Selah ---

I AM that I AM, and ever shall be

SO - I AM

Solen Aum Solen

Recorded by Sister Thedra of the Emerald Cross

Be Not Deceived

Know ye this: There is but One "Lord of Lords" - One "Host of Hosts" and One Sananda -- Yet it is now come when many shall come declaring that they are He-- That they are the Lord of Lords - "<u>THE</u> Host of Hosts" - and "THE Sananda" ---

Yet I say unto thee: - They shall be revealed for that which they are For I say unto thee: I Am not mocked -- While they would deceive "the elect" - I say unto thee: I have given unto thee Mine WORD -- Mine hand have I given unto thee --

I have given unto thee the <u>power</u> and the AUTHORITY to speak in MINE NAME - and I have put MINE WORDS into thine mouth - and thou hast spoken THEM IN MINE NAME -- And at no time hast thou plundered the storehouse of the willfull - and the ones which THINK themself wise ---

I say unto thee: Thou art within the Law - to give unto them that which I give unto thee for them -- And at no time hast thou given unto them any false word - for I bear witness of that which ye do - and I know that which I say -- And it is given unto Me to see them plunder and pilfer the words of others - for the sake of <u>appearing wise</u>! ---

I say unto them: Be ye not so foolish as to pilfer Mine Word - or disturb It -- Change not a Word! And give credit where credit is due ---

Be ye as the ones which hast prepared thineself to receive Mine Word - for it carries with It Great POWER ---

I AM the Lord of Hosts -

I AM the Lord God -

I AM Sananda

Recorded by Sister Thedra of the Emerald Cross

They Have Sold Their Birthright

Beloved Ones -- There are many which are downcast/ downtrodden - and weary of body and mind -- I say unto them: "Hold ye steadfast - for I Am with thee unto the end" ---

I Am come that there be Light - yet there is great darkness within <u>the world of men</u> ---

While they run after strange gods - and the "Midas touch" - I say they are as ants which have been displaced -- They are running hither and yon - knowing not where to go - or why -- Yet they ask of themself <u>where</u>? - where? - why? -- Yet they ask not of the Father -- They are consistent in their question - where? - where can I find peace? - where can I find security? - where can I find safety? ---

Yet I say unto them - there is NO PEACE WITHIN THEM -- They have not established it within themself -- They have squandered their inheritance - they have sold their birthright for a pittance -- Now I say unto them - their cries shall go out thru all the lands of the Earth and they shall echo back upon their ears ---

I say it is given unto Me to Know the wonton of these -- They have gone their <u>own way</u> - heeding not the Law which is given into them -- They give not of themself that there be Peace within the world of men They make of the Earth their footstool - despoiling Her - and being unto Her much torment -- I say She shall throw them off Her back -- She shall no longer give unto them food and a resting place -- She shall no longer be unto them the "Mother" -- She shall no longer comfort and nourish them -- For it is given unto Her to be freed from Her bondage also - She too shall be freed - even as the Children of God - as the "Sons of God" -- For as She hast waited long - She shall now find Her waiting shall end - and it shall be a Victorious ending --

So be it I speak that they which have ears to hear MIGHT HEAR.

So Be It - I AM

Sananda

Recorded by Sister Thedra of the Emerald Cross

The Remnant
Emissaries - Messengers - Trail Blazers

Sori Sori -- Hold ye steadfast! Be ye as ones prepared for the Greater Part -- For I say unto thee - it is now come when it shall be necessary to put on the WHOLE "ARMOR OF GOD" -- For it is given unto thee to be part of the "Remnant" -- The "Remnant shall be gathered together and they shall be given a <u>mighty</u> work -- They shall be as the Ones prepared for their part -- They shall KNOW WELL their parts - for this are they NOW being prepared ---

While they know not all the other parts - they shall work in One accord - unto <u>one</u> end - that of Oneness - One purpose - One for ALL - for the GOOD OF ALL---

They shall be selfless in their serving - and ask of no man awards - They shall be as the "Servants of the Most High Living God" -- They shall be humble of spirit - and walk as one of the Initiates -- They shall be known for their work/ "By Their Fruit" ---

No man shall set foot against these which are sent that they do 'this mighty work' -- I Am come that they be brought out of bondage and prepared -- So be it that I Am come for to lift them up -- While they but walk one step at a time - seeing not the fullness of the Plan - they <u>know</u> that which they are about -- They have been well schooled -- So be it that <u>these</u> are the Messengers/ the Emissaries and Mine hands/ Mine feet - made manifest -- I say unto thee - these are the "Hope" of the NEW DAY -- These are the "Trail Blazers"-- These are the "Pioneers" So be it I Am the DIRECTOR of this New Dispensation - and I am not to be discounted - or put into a corner - for I KNOW what I Am about!

I KNOW WELL Mine Part and I shall finish it - and return unto Mine Father which hast sent Me --

I AM Sananda

Recorded by Sister Thedra of the Emerald Cross

Hail Unto the New Dawn
Mother Eternal

Beloved: It is now come when ye shall give unto them this Word - and it shall profit them to heed that which I say -- It is from the beginning that man hast set himself apart - as separate from Me the Lord God - and it is <u>not</u> so - for he is not separate from Me - for I AM the ONE -- I AM the SUM TOTAL of ALL that man shall <u>ever</u> BE - ALL that he shall become ---

I say - man is not a thing apart -- He could not have existence apart from ME - for I AM That Which hast sent him forth - and <u>he</u> hast cut himself off from Me / in his THINKING/ BY his thinking -- He knows not that he is "THE MAN" of Mine Imaging -- He hast had his memory blanked from him ---

Now he shall weary of his <u>sleep</u> - and he shall become restless - and his sleep shall be disturbed - and he shall awaken with a Great Light.

Too - let it be said - that Great Light shall flood the Earth -- For this have I sent Mine Sons unto the Earth - that there be a Great Awakening It is now time for this New Awakening - and it shall be the Glorious New Dawn -- Hail unto the New Day - for I say unto thee - it shall bring with it Great Light -- And it shall be the JOY of MINE HEART -- Such is Mine Joy when Mine Children return unto Me --

LET IT BE - for I AM thine

Mother Eternal

Recorded by Sister Thedra of the Emerald Cross

THOU ART OF THE 'FIRST BORN'

Beloved Ones -- This day it shall become known that there are Ones which have ascended unto Me in <u>all</u> <u>their</u> <u>Glory</u> ---

There are Ones Which have finished their sojourn within flesh - to return unto it NO MORE -- While these which have returned unto Me - are as One with Me - I say unto thee - they are no less part of thee -- For art thou not of ME - born in the fashion which I didst image? ---

Hast it not been said that thou art of the "First Born"? -- IT IS SO - thou art of the "First Born" ---

Now it is come when thou shall stand face to face with THINE SELF - and ye shall KNOW thineself to BE "Immortal Beings" - and no man shall deny thee ---

So be it that there is not one which enter into the INNER TEMPLE without the aid of Them Which hast gone before them ---

I have sent Mine SONS unto thee that ye might be prepared to enter in -- Straight is the Way - and narrow is the Gate - for I have prepared it - and I AM HE Which hast given unto thee Being -- I have sent thee forth as Mine hand made manifest upon the Earth -- And I have endowed unto thee LIFE - LIFE of MINE LIFE-- And no man shall deprive thee of thine SONSHIP ---

So be it - I say unto thee - enter into the Place of MINE ABODE - and be ye as One returned unto thine <u>rightful</u> <u>abode</u> -- And receive of Me thine Crown --

And no more shall ye go out --

I AM thine Father Eternal -

> **Recorded by Sister Thedra of the Emerald Cross**

The Order of The First Born

Sons of God art thou -- Thou <u>art</u> of the First Born - and it is given unto Me to be One of This Order -- While all are not of the Same Order - I say unto thee thou art of This Order of The First Born -- While thou hast not remembered thine inheritance - thine Lineage I say unto thee - thou art of the Father Born -- Sent forth as His Emissaries - as His Sons -- And at no time shall any man deprive thee of thine Inheritance -- So be it - it is a "Princely" One---

Let it be said that ye shall come to <u>know</u> as I <u>know</u> -- So let it suffice that I Am the Lord thy God --

Be ye blest of Me and by Me --

I AM Sananda

> **Recorded by Sister Thedra of the Emerald Cross**

Their Crime Against Themself

This day I would say unto thee - let them BE - let them BE - and give unto "<u>them</u>" no power <u>over</u> <u>thee</u> -- Ask not for their opinion or favors -

Give credit where credit is due ---

I say unto thee - these which sit in high places and usurp the power allotted unto them <u>are</u> <u>the</u> <u>traitors</u> -- They have betrayed their trust - AND themself -- They have despoiled the ones which have looked unto "them" for help and assistance ---

While it is given unto Me to <u>Know</u> the true from the false - <u>they</u> have given themself over to greed and crime -- They have committed first a crime against <u>themself</u> - and the people of the lands of the Earth They are want to put their fingers in the till of ALL peoples -- They are not want to lift up the people -- They are want to take unto themself <u>great</u> <u>glory</u> and <u>gain</u> ---

I say unto <u>them</u>: "These are thine BROTHERS - that ye are so prone to persecute/ plunder/ rob/ subject and fortune unto great suffering -- Thou hast taken upon thineself great responsibility - which thou shall assume unto the last mile -- The last farthing shall ye pay for thine foolishness"-- I say: Time shall not eradicate the history of thine work or deeds/ thine persecutions/ thine hypocrisy" -- Let it be said that "<u>Time</u>" shall not release thee from thine debts which thou hast accrued So be ye mindful of the Law - and transgress It no more! ---

Hear ye Me - and be ye as Ones prepared - for I say unto thee - that which ye send out shall surely and <u>truly</u> return unto thee as "BREAD UPON THE WATERS"---

It behooves thee to take notice of that which I say unto thee - for I Am not a fool -- I AM the Lord thy God - Son of GOD THE FATHER Sent that there BE LIGHT --

So be it I speak unto thee that ye might <u>know</u> the LAW --

I AM HE Which IS COME -

Sananda

Recorded by Sister Thedra of the Emerald Cross

Man / The Mighty Presence

Soran Speaking -- It is given unto Me to <u>know</u> the way of man -- While I Am not within flesh - neither have "I" taken unto Mineself flesh at <u>any</u> <u>time</u> - I know that which flesh <u>is</u>/ the way of flesh/ the trials and tribulations/ limitations ---

Yet it is clearly and surely written that flesh is not "man" -- Man but commands the flesh -- He takes unto himself the substance of Earth for such a vehicle of flesh - which <u>is</u> <u>his</u> for a duration of a given time. This time is given unto him when he comes into flesh -- It is known unto him - the <u>time</u>/ the day/ the moment - of his release -- Yet he hast taken up the flesh for a purpose - and he hast made a <u>covenant</u> that the purpose be fulfilled -- Now let it be understood that when he does not fulfill that covenant - when he rebels against the covenant which <u>he</u> made with "THE PRESENCE" of <u>his</u> <u>own</u> <u>Being</u> - he betrays <u>himself</u> - NONE OTHER ---

I say unto thee: The hour is known unto his ALL-WISE PRESENCE -- The hour is his own choice - granted unto him from the beginning -- The way is provided - and it is his choice -- For that matter there are no mysteries unto HIS PRESENCE - for the PRESENCE is ever present - and when he turns his back on "HIS" PRESENCE he but cuts himself off from the Source of "HIS BEING" in <u>thinking</u> himself a separate thing - a thing apart/ separate from the ONENESS OF HIS BEING ---

This is not a mystery! This is not new/ a new Doctrine/ a strange doctrine -- It is so spoken from the beginning - and "man" hast chosen to go his own way - hearing not that which hast been said -- Let it be understood - that the time draws nigh when they shall stand face to face with THE PRESENCE Which they are so prone to forget ---

Let it be -- For this it is said: Be true unto thineself -- And as it is written - So Be It --

I AM Soran

Recorded by Sister Thedra of the Emerald Cross

Mine Own Creation

Mine Beloved Children -- Have I not known thee for that which thou art? -- For that which THOU ART - I have created from out Mine Own Substance -- I have sent thee forth as MINE OWN CREATION - from out MINE OWN BEING - as part of Mineself -- For no other Substance shall be equal unto MINE -- NO OTHER SUBSTANCE can endure - for I AM the Substance of LIFE ETERNAL - and EVERLASTING AM I -- And for this I say unto thee: "THOU ART ETERNAL BEINGS" - and none shall deprive thee of thine Eternal Inheritance -- So be it that I have given unto thee the SONSHIP which is thine - and no man shall rob thee of that! ---

I speak unto thee as thine Father Eternal - for from ME hast thou come into thine Eternal Being -- And by MINE WILL hast thou been given Divine Custody of MINE SOBRIETIES -- and I have entrusted thee with MINE LAWS/ MINE SCRIPTS/ MINE WORD - Which is HOLY/ PURE - and within Itself SUFFICIENT unto thine Salvation - I say unto thee - I AM SUFFICIENT unto thee - and <u>nothing</u> shall separate thee from ME - for I AM the SOURCE of thine BEING - and nothing shall deprive thee of BEING ---

I say - thine BEING is that which is DIVINE and ONE WITH ME Give unto ME credit for KNOWING thee - as I KNOW MINESELF.

So be it I abide within the ALL - ALL IS - and for this I say unto thee - That which IS - and EVER SHALL BE is MINE - Worlds without end - and at no time shall MINE CREATION be destroyed ---

Let it be said: "Change there shall be - yet the REAL shall remain UNTOUCHED/ UNHARMED"---

So be it - I AM - and I shall ALWAYS BE --

So be ye at Peace and Poise --

For this I speak unto thee thusly --

I AM THE ALL-

SOLEN AUM SOLEN

Recorded by Sister Thedra of the Emerald Cross

Fear Not!

Beloved Ones -- Let this day bring unto thee fulfillment of ALL the SCRIPTS - ALL the HOLY WORD -- For I say unto thee - this is the day of <u>fulfillment</u> -- This is the "End Times"/ the time of the end - when it shall be finished - and <u>done</u>! - to be repeated <u>no</u> more -- So let it BE as the Father hast willed it ---

Hasten ye to meet <u>this</u> day with gladness -- Greet the NEW day and fear not!! - For it is now come when ye shall have great assistance -- For this have WE the "MIGHTY HOST" revealed Ourself unto thee.

Let it be understood that the Way is now made clear that ye be delivered out -- And it behooves thee to make ready thineself to receive Our Assistance - and at no time shall We deceive thee ---

I say unto thee - I AM Come that ye might know the true from the false -- So be it I AM the Lord thy God - sent of Mine Father that there be Light -- So let it BE ---

While I say there IS LIGHT - I say unto thee: "BE ye ONE WITH IT -- Walk ye therein and fear NOT!

I AM with thee unto the end - which shall be thine Victory ---

I AM Sananda

Recorded by Sister Thedra of the Emerald Cross

Order of Melchezedeck: The Law - The Council

Beloved of Mine Being: Say unto them: - There is no law which binds the one which hast been eliberated from ALL bondage - for they are FREE -- They become the law - therefore they are not bound by it ---

They are one with the "ALL" -- They need no law - for they transcend ALL Earth laws - such as the attraction of the Moon - and the gravitation of the Earth -- They are no longer under such law - for they are above these laws which belong unto the realm of Earth ---

While it is within the power of the Mighty Council to give unto them passport - they shall earn it -- There is NO short path -- The "Passport" shall be earned!

At no time shall these laws be nullified or set aside - in favor of any people - nation - or part of any people or nation ---

I say - the law is valid - and shall be as it hast been - It shall not be broken without dire consequence -- While they are wont to nullify the law of gravitation - it is the long way round ---

I say it is the LONG way - and it carries with it great trials - frustration - and hardship ---

I say unto them - "LOOK UP"! - See the first Light which is given unto thee - which still shines within the heavens - and know ye that there is a LAW governing ALL THINGS! -- It shall NOT be nullified! for IT IS THE CAUSE of thine BEING ---

So be it I have spoken - and I Am not finished --- I shall speak again and again - for I Am come that ye might know the wisdom which is thine for the preparation -- Therefore it is said MANY times: "Prepare thineself for the Greater Part" ---

I AM One of the Mighty Council -

I AM One of the Sibors -

I AM of the Order of Melchezedeck

Recorded by Sister Thedra of the Emerald Cross

In Great Victory!

Beloved of Mine Being -- Hast it not been said that thou art of the Order of Melchezedek? I say unto thee it is <u>so</u> -- So be it that I AM of this Order - and I KNOW - for I Am the Priest of the "Inner Temple" - set apart as the "MOST WORTHY GRAND MASTER" - the part of which there is none other so designated -- It is fortuned unto thee to be on this Order - for yea - a time and a time - and a half a time - for it is not as yet done - it is not finished - time is not ENDED ---

I say unto thee:- Ye shall come into the FULLNESS of TIME - and ye shall know <u>time</u> as no more - for <u>thine</u> time is but an illusion -- It is but as the twinkling of an eye unto US -- That which ye call "A LIFE TIME" - yea as the twinkling of the eye – For We see the records from the time of thine going out - until thine return -- We see thine sojourn as finished now -- Finished it shall be - and I say unto thee - in Great Victory! -- For it shall end in the Victorious accomplishment of thine return -- Return ye shall-- I say REJOICE THIS DAY that it is SO -- So let Us Rejoice together ---

I AM Sanat Kumara

Recorded by Sister Thedra of the Emerald Cross

The Order of Melchezedeck
Sanandas Testimony

Be ye as Ones prepared to receive that which I shall give unto thee - and it shall be given unto them as I give it unto thee -- For <u>no</u> <u>word</u> <u>is</u> <u>to</u> <u>be</u> <u>changed</u> - <u>or</u> <u>added</u> <u>to</u> - <u>or</u> <u>taken</u> <u>away</u> -- For I Am come unto thee that they might have this Mine Word - and it shall profit them which receive it unto themself - for they shall be blest thereby ---

Let it be known that I Am come - that I have gone out from the Inner Temple - that the world of men might be as nought -- That which man hast fortuned unto the Earth - it shall be no more -- Yet I say that each and every one hast the responsibility of his own acts/ actions/ deeds/ words - and the harvest thereof -- For as the fowls of the air - the deeds shall return unto their breeding place -- Let it be known that none escape the law! --

So be it that I come that the Order of Melchezedeck be established upon the Earth - for It is of the <u>Higher</u> <u>Order</u> than that of man - that which man hast fashioned -- For it is of the Highest Order that man can conceive - and it is fashioned for his benefit -- For the Initiate shall come into the fullness of his Estate through the Order of Melchezedeck - and at no time shall any other Order equal that of this One -- For it is the Order which was from the beginning - and It hast not been put asunder by man's darkness/ or unknowing ---

I say unto thee - thou art of the Order of Melchezedeck - and none shall put his foot against thee - for there is A "HOST" Which stands ready to assist thee-- Be ye as Ones which hear that which I say unto thee - and walk ye with head high - and I shall give unto thee of Mine Cup -- I bid thee drink ye to the full-- And be ye blest as I have been blest ---

So be it I speak unto thee at this Altar - that ye might record that which I say that it might go into the Record for all which follow after thee -- So let it be known that I have borne testimony of thee this day.

I AM the Lord thy God

Sananda

Recorded by Sister Thedra of the Emerald Cross

Sananda's Invitation

Behold ye this day the Handiwork of the Lord - The Lord God - The Host of Hosts -- See ye the Word made manifest -- Know ye that there IS POWER in the "WORD"-- THE WORD hast proceeded out Mine Mouth: Let there BE LIGHT - and THERE IS LIGHT! -- Walk ye therein - and be ye blest - as I have been blest -- So be it that I have been blest of MINE FATHER Which hast sent ME---

Now it is come when I bid thee enter into MINE PLACE OF ABODE - and rest ye assured that none enter unprepared -- For this is it said: "Prepare Thine Self for The Greater Part" -- So be it I have come unto thee that ye be blest even as I -- SO LET IT BE ---

I AM The Lord God -

Sananda

Recorded by Sister Thedra of the Emerald Cross

Concerning the Temple to be Established

Sori Sori -- Let it be known that the Way hast been made clear before thee - and the door swings both ways-- We enter into thine place of abode - and bid thee enter into OURS (The Mighty Host)

While it is so - We have said: "None enter unprepared" -- So be it the Truth ---

While it is said: "None enter Unprepared" - I say many stand ready to assist thee -- So be it that We of the Host - have been prepared for this day - when We might give assistance ---

It is said: "Be ye as Pillars of the Temple - for there are some which would enter in - which are not FIT timber" -- These shall be cast out and shall have no part in the building of THE TEMPLE - which shall be builded within the Earth - wherein the Father's Kingdom shall be set up --- And at no time shall WE be caught off guard -- We see and know the material which shall go into the building of HIS TEMPLE - Which shall stand forever and a day -- So be it that I have spoken unto thee that they might know that which I have said concerning the TEMPLE OF THE MIGHTY COUNCIL - The ORDER OF MELCHEZEDECK So let them have thee Record which shall profit them to KNOW - and TO KNOW is WISDOM-- So be it and Selah ---

I AM The High Priest in This Temple -

I AM Sananda

Recorded by Sister Thedra

The Return of the Prodigal Son

Beloved of Mine Being -- I have given unto thee the Part which is Mine to give - and it is now become necessary to give unto thee this Word -- Let it be for the GOOD of ALL -- So be it ye shall be blest to give it unto them which have a mind to receive it ---

It is given unto Me to be the "Most Worthy Grand Master of the Inner Temple" - and I say unto thee: "The Door" is now ajar - and I bid thee enter into the Holy of Holies -- I bid thee pass -- For <u>this</u> have I prepared the Way before thee -- The Altar stands foursquare -- The Flame burns high - and the Host of Hosts bid thee enter -- I say unto thee: "The Door Stands Ajar" and none shall close it before thee -- It shall open wide before thee as ye enter near --

I tell thee - many shall receive thee unto themself - with the glad Hosannas - and a Great Cry of Joy shall ring out -- Blest are they which have Won their Victory -- Blest are they which have returned unto their Abiding Place -- For it shall be a Glad Gathering in - a Glad Return -- Let the Glad Tidings peal out - HAIL! HAIL! unto the VICTOR! -- THE SON HAST RETURNED! -- So be it and Selah--

I Am come that it be a Victorious Reunion --

So let it BE --

I AM Sanat Kumara

> **Recorded by Sister Thedra of the Emerald Cross**

Pass Ye In

Behold this day the Power of THE WORD -- Know ye that IT IS the SUBSTANCE of that which is MADE MANIFEST ---

I say: The POWER of THE WORD is THE SUBSTANCE of the manifest ---

Now ye shall give unto this GREAT CONCERN - and PONDER this MINE WORD ---

When it is come that the DOOR SWINGS WIDE before thee - THE WORD shall be put into thine mouth - and none shall be unto thee a BARRIER - for no man shall bar thine way -- I say NO MAN shall keep thee out - for ye shall HAVE THE WORD -- And IT shall be as the "Power which shall move mountains" ---

While THE WORD is yet not revealed unto them which have NOT entered into the INNER TEMPLE - IT SHALL BE! - and it shall suffice them - for it is sufficient into its own - and nothing can be added to - or taken away - for IT is complete within ITSELF -- IT shall go forth as a MIGHTY ROD of STRENGTH - as A POWER GREATER than ANYTHING MAN HAST KNOWN BEFORE! -- I say: <u>BEHOLD!!!</u>

THE POWER OF THE WORD - and enter ye into THE HOLY OF HOLIES --

So be it I say unto thee - PASS YE IN and REJOICE FOREVERMORE ---

So be it I AM Sananda

Recorded by Sister Thedra of the Emerald Cross

"The Zealots" "Preachments" "Example"

Beloved Ones__ This day let it be said that the Way is clear before thee and no man shall bar thine way -- Yet it is given unto thee to choose the way in which ye shall go -- And at no time shall ye be unto another a barrier - for he too hast free will - and he too shall find his way -- It is the Way of the Initiate to give unto each as he is prepared to receive Yet the zealot <u>gives</u> that which is designed for <u>him</u> -- He gives unto the foolish - and therefore fortunes unto himself <u>great</u> <u>sorrow</u> and stress -- He grieves for the ones which heed not HIS preachments - and besets himself for his rejection ---

Now it is come when the zealots shall see the folly of their "Preachments" -- They shall walk in THE WAY I POINT - giving of themself that ALL might SEE the Light -- Yet it shall be given unto them which have an eye to see - to follow the Light -- They shall know him by his "light" - and no man shall impose upon another his opinions or preconceived ideas -- He shall be unto them a shining light - a lamp unto their feet - walking in Mine footsteps - and giving that which he IS -- And his light shall NOT be hidden ---

This is the "Path of the Initiate" - and at no time shall a Candidate be denied - when he hast prepared himself to receive -- For it is the LAW "As ye are prepared - so shall ye receive" -- Let it be the "Greater Part" ---

So be it I have spoken unto them which would be unto their Brothers - their keepers -- I say: Let thine light so shine that they might see it and follow thee ---

So be it that I AM the Lord thy God

Sananda

Recorded by Sister Thedra of the Emerald Cross

Blessed are They

Blessed are they which come unto this Altar ---

Blessed are they which hear that which I say ---

Blessed are they which receive of Me - for they shall KNOW ME.

Blessed are they which give of themself - for their reward shall be Great ---

Blessed are they which ask of the Father - for they shall receive ---

Blessed are they which KNOW ME - for they shall KNOW MINE FATHER which hast SENT ME ---

Blessed are they which KNOW MINE FATHER - for they shall abide with ME forever ---

Blessed are they which abide with Me - for they shall go out no more ---

Blessed are they WHICH ABIDE WITH ME - for they SHALL GO OUT NO MORE!! ---

So be it I Am come that they might become One with Me - and Mine Father and I ARE ONE ---

So be it I AM Sananda

Recorded by Sister Thedra of the Emerald Cross

The Council of Twelve Lights
School of Melchezedeck

Say unto "them" - there are many which sit in HIGH PLACES - which are alert unto the way of man -- For These are the Ones which are sent that the CROOKED be made straight ---

I say: The MIGHTY COUNCIL holds forth for the purpose of setting straight - that which has been <u>made</u> <u>crooked</u> ---

They are in no wise <u>imposters</u> -- They are NOT asleep -- Yet they are of the mind to set straight that which hast been MADE CROOKED!.

So be it that the time draws nigh when it shall be straightened - for "THE COUNCIL" sleeps not - neither does IT go into lethargy -- For it is given unto IT to be made up of the SONS OF GOD - which have the RIGHT and the AUTHORITY - to do that which is given unto Them to do -- THEY ARE COME ! - closer unto the Earth at this time that there be Greater Light - more STRENGTH -- And a greater number of people hast been alerted -- And these shall be given INSTRUCTIONS in THE WAY OF THE INITIATE --

And it behooves them to APPLY themself diligently -- For it is now come when the END TIME is as a fleeting moment -- Soon shall it be no more - and then the Initiate shall KNOW that which he hast done/ accomplished - and he shall stand free - and KNOW/ SEE that which hast been accomplished through and by the COUNCIL OF THE TWELVE LIGHTS -- The Council of the Twelve Lights are AS ONE MAN -- They are not divided against themself -- They are One of mind and purpose -- They are not dissuaded -- They are not want to turn aside.

They are of the SCHOOL OF MELCHEZEDECK - and THEY KNOW WELL Their Part --- For this have They been prepared -- So be it I Am the Head of this School - the Head of this GREAT AUGUST BODY - and I KNOW that which I say unto thee ---

So let it suffice that I Am the Lord of Lords -

Host of Hosts --

I AM Sananda

Recorded by Sister Thedra of the Emerald Cross

I am the Forerunner of Thineself

Beloved Ones -- This is Mine day - Mine time - and I say unto thee - it is given unto ME to KNOW the TIME/ the day - for I Am the Lord thy God - and it is given unto Me to KNOW - yea - even unto the "Last Day"---

While it is given unto thee to know NOT THE HOUR! I Am come that ye might come to KNOW even as I ---

I Am the One sent that ye MIGHT KNOW - for I Am the forerunner of thineself -- I come before thee -- I go before - that the Way be prepared before thee - that ye might make thine ascent in the way in which I have gone -- I say that ye might make thine return - even as I have made Mine -- So be it that no man shall be unto thee a barrier -- No man shall stay thine flight -- And at no time shall ye be denied thine entrance into of the Place of Mine Abode -- I have asked of thee obedience unto the LAW -- I have given unto thee the LAWS - and thou hast been forthright in thine ways -- And it is given unto Me to see thine strivings - and thine Work --

Yet I say unto thee - be ye vigilant - and ask of no man ought -- Give unto NO MAN power to dissuade thee And ask of NO MAN his blessing or his opinion -- So be it that I Am come that ye be sufficient unto thineself -- Yet it is not as yet done -- For this do I give unto thee MINE HAND - that ye be Self-sufficient -I say unto thee: COME YE - follow ye ME - and I shall lead thee into Mine Place of Abode -- So be it I say unto thee: Let it BE as the Father hast WILLED it -- And at no time shall ye be denied entrance ---

Come - Let Us rejoice together --

I AM Sananda

Recorded by Sister Thedra of the Emerald Cross

The Passport Earned

Beloved Ones -- Say unto them that the Way is opened up before them and they which prepare themself to enter into MINE PLACE OF ABODE shall not be denied admittance ---

So be it that their passport is: "Their Preparation" -- I KNOW them and that which is necessary for their preparation - I KNOW their weakness -- I KNOW wherein their strength ABOUNDS -- And at no time shall that strength be diminished! ---

So be it that I have sent thee forth - as Mine hand thrust forth -- And I have given unto thee the power to do that which I have given unto thee to do -- And at no time shall I deny thee - the strength to do the work which is MINE - that which is necessary UNTO MINE WORK.

When it is finished - I shall withdraw Mine hand - and I shall give unto thee a Part - unlike that which thou hast known -- I shall do THIS AND MORE! ---

I shall bring thee into the Place of Mine Abode and I shall say unto thee: "WELL DONE - MINE SERVANT - BE YE AS ONE WHICH HAST EARNED THINE PASSPORT INTO THIS PLACE"-- And ye shall be seated upon Mine Right hand - and ye shall sup with Me -- And ye shall counsel with Me - and We shall be about THE FATHER'S BUSINESS -- And We shall be glad that it IS COME when thou hast returned unto thine rightful Estate -- So be it that I Am come that this be accomplished THIS DAY --

So be it I AM

Sananda

Recorded by Sister Thedra of the Emerald Cross

There is But One Lord God

Beloved of Mine Being:

This I would say unto thee this day -- There is but ONE LORD GOD - the ONE SENT that there be LIGHT in the world of men ---

Now it is come when The Word - Which hast proceeded out of His Mouth - shall be manifest -- And it shall be <u>Known</u> that He - The Lord of Lords - The Host of Hosts - Sibor of Sibors - shall be as the One through which ye enter into the Holy of Holies - and none other.-

I say they search - they look for signs and wonders - yet they FIND HIM NOT - for they seek after THINGS/ SIGNS/ WONDERS/ MATERIAL GAIN - and they are not aware of HIS PRESENCE - for they are blinded by their own <u>Awful</u> -- They are wont to give unto HIM credit for Being that Which HE IS ---

Be ye as One blest this day -- Be ye blest by Mine Presence -- For this do I speak this day ---

So Be It I AM

Sanat Kumara

Recorded by Sister Thedra of the Emerald Cross

O Father! Thy Will Be Done

Most Holy Father - Father of Us which have come out from Thee -- Thou ART the GIVER of ALL which IS - and ever shall BE - for THOU ART the SOURCE OF OUR BEING---

TO YOU O Father - We give ALL the Glory - ALL the Credit for that which We ARE-- That which we shall BECOME is by THINE GRACE and MERCY ---

So be it that We are but Thine Hand - reached out as an extension of Thine Self -- That which We ARE is but Thine Own Self - reached out as Thine Hand---

Cause Us to use it as Thou would have Us use Thine Hand - for that which YOU would do -- And let Us have the Mind and the Strength to endure all the sorrows of men - all the grief - all the misfortune - which is so much part of man's fortune - which they have brought about for their own lack of memory - which they have forfeited -- So be it I speak unto Thee this day - that they might KNOW that Which I AM -- That which I say unto Thee O Father - is that which Thou Knowest -- Yet "they" know not Our Relationship ---

Let them come to KNOW - even as I KNOW ---

So Be It I AM Thine Son

Sananda

Recorded by Sister Thedra of the Emerald Cross

One in Thine Midst

Beloved Ones -- This day let this Word be recorded in the language which they might comprehend - that they might KNOW that which I say unto thee ---

This shall be sufficient unto this day - and shall be unto them which receive It - Great Light ---

There is now come into thine midst - One which hast not been with thee before -- He hast not been of the Earth - and never shall He be of the Earth - for He is One above the Earth - and He hast gone out for the purpose of giving of Himself - that certain things be accomplished THIS DAY -- He shall be Great Light unto the peoples of ALL the Earth - for He hast brought with Him Great Wisdom - Great Love - and Knowlege of all the "Ways of man" and his wants/ his frailties/ and his capabilities --

His wants are only that man be lifted up -- He shall ask of man nothing save obedience unto the Law -- He shall walk as One ILLUMINATED/ as An Initiate - and He shall NOT betray Himself OR His trust - for He shall be true unto Himself -- He shall be as One Which hast Great Opposition - yet the opposers shall be put down - and He shall not fail in His Mission -- He hast not been born of woman of Earth - for He hast not come as a "babe" -- He hast not come as out of the East -- He hast come as One prepared to do battle with the "dragon"

He is well fortified - for He carries with Him the "Sword of Truth and Justice" -- He wears the "Armor of God" -- And He holds within His Hand the Orb and The Scepter - for He is the "Favorite Son" -- He hast the Power which is endowed unto Him of The Father Which hast Sent Him –

So be it I say unto thee - hold out thine hand- and He shall give unto thee as thou art prepared to receive of Him - for He KNOWS thine capacity ---

So be it He now walks amongst thee unknown for the most part/ uncrowned/ unsung -- For He hast come as a thief in the night -- The darkness hangs thick about them - and they see not for they have as yet not awakened unto HIS PRESENCE -- For this have they stumbled in darkness - knowing not that there IS LIGHT ---

I say unto them - Awaken Thineself - and be ye Aware of that which goes on about thee ---

Be ye blest this day -- For this do I speak ---

I AM THE NAMELESS ONE

                  Recorded by Sister Thedra of the Emerald Cross

Thoughtfulness & Gratitude

Beloved Children -- Children of Mine own boson - I say unto thee this day - it is Mine Part to give unto thee of Mine Self that ye have thine BEING -- I say - it is of Me that thou art sustained - for from ME dost thou take thine Sustenance -- While thou knowest not that which I AM - I AM thine Mother - from Whose Breast thou hast been nurtured - and from Which thou hast been fed -- I tell thee thou hast taken thine part from Me - wherein thou hast been as Ones prepared to give unto others - that which thou hast taken from ME ---

I say unto thee - take no credit unto thineself for that which thou hast taken from Me - for it is Mine to give -- And it is the part of the unknowing ones to take without thought of the Source from which it cometh ---

I say unto thee Mine Children - be ye mindful of ME thine Mother for I Am the Mother through which ALL Manifestation cometh -- So be it that I Am mindful of Mine Creation - for I Am not alone in this - for I Am ONE with that which I bring into manifestation - and I forget it not -- Be ye as Ones blest this day -- Walk ye as Ones thoughtful - and as Ones prepared to receive in Greater Measure ---

I AM thine

Mother Eternal

Recorded by Sister Thedra of the Emerald Cross

Behold Ye Mine Sons - The Hand of God Moveth

Behold ye Mine Sons - the Hand of God moveth -- It moveth in ways ye know not of -- I say unto thee - Behold ye - - SEE THE HAND OF GOD MOVE ---

KNOW YE that IT MOVETH -- Hear ye that which is said unto thee -- And be ye as Ones <u>Alert</u> - and fret not for the morrow -- For I say unto thee - Mine Sons - that THIS DAY thou shall abide in Mine House -- Thou shall stand within MINE PRESENCE - and ye shall KNOW ME - and ye shall be GLAD -- So be it I speak unto thee which have given unto ME - ear -- For thou hast come into the age of accountability - and thou art <u>now</u> the Sons of God - wherein thou shall receive thine Inheritance ---

Thou hast groveled for a pittance -- Thou hast fed upon the husks - Now I shall prepare a table within thine midst - and ye shall partake thereof and be fed - and nourished -- SO BE IT I speak unto thee as thine Father Solen Aum Solen ---

So BE it I AM thine

Eternal Parent

Recorded By Sister Thedra of the Emerald Cross

Wherein Have I Denied thee?

Be ye as Mine Hand - and give unto them THIS Mine Word - that they might profit thereby ---

Say unto them - as I would say: that - it is now come - when Great shall be the suffering and confusion -- Great shall be THE LIGHT -- Great shall be THE ASSISTANCE THROUGH THE LIGHT -- And all which turn unto IT shall be given assistance - for none shall be denied ---

NONE SHALL BE DENIED!

I say: -- For the GOOD OF ALL - do WE WORK WITHOUT CEASING ---

While they sleep - WE of THE MIGHTY COUNCIL WORK -- "WE" Work while they dream the dreams which torment them/ while they run hither and yon - fearing that which shall come upon them ---

I say unto thee: "Fear Not! for I AM COME that ye have the comprehension/ the KNOWLEGE of that which "IS" / that which shall BE"-- And when it is said: "Be ye as ONE WITH ME" - wherein have I failed thee? -- Wherein have I denied thee? ---

Is it not said: that - as ye are prepared - so shall ye receive? -- So let it be - and give unto ME credit for KNOWING thee! - for I see thee as thou ART-- I know thee - and thine capacity -- So be it I give not unto the unjust -- I give not unto the wonton - that they MISUSE ME! -- I say they are not of "MINE FOLD" -- They are wont to follow Me -- They have not asked of Me -- They cry out for mercy - yet they ask of STRANGE GODS - their <u>idols</u> -- They make a mockery of Mine Words While they deny Me - and that which I AM - that which I give unto them for their sake/ that they be returned unto their rightful estate ---

I come not to give unto them lengthy discourses for their entertainment/ amusement ---

I AM about Mine Fathers Business - I KNOW their needs/ I KNOW their wants/ their strength/ their capacity -- Too - I KNOW their frailties/ their every deed/ word/ and all their days I shall KNOW! - for I Am not asleep!---

I AM the Lord thy God - Sananda

Recorded by Sister Thedra of the Emerald Cross

The Darkness Comprehends Not the Light

Sori Sori--

Have I not given unto thee <u>this day</u>? Have I not given unto thee that which hast sustained thee? Have I not led thee - and been unto thee thine shield and thine buckler? -- So be it I Am THE ONE SENT that there BE LIGHT -- So be it that I AM THE LORD GOD - Sent that there BE LIGHT -- So let IT BE ---

Now it is come when the sleepers shall come forth - as ones which have long been asleep -- They shall see and hear - and ask wherein they are/ wherein they have been -- They shall ask in wonderment - knowing not that they have slept -- For that matter they KNOW NOT!! -- They neither know wherein they are staid - neither do they know wherein they goeth -- They KNOW NOT - that they have been portioned the sad lot/ that of the sleeper --

I say unto them - AWAKEN -- And they shall stir themself - and they shall be as ones which have ears to hear - and they shall listen unto Mine SONG -- For I shall sing it out from the Mountain Top - and it shall sound upon the ETH as a String Lute - and none shall deny ME - for I Am that I AM ---

I AM the ONE Which hast Gone forth as a Light in the darkness - yet the darkness comprehends NOT THE LIGHT.

I AM Sananda

Recorded by Sister Thedra of the Emerald Cross

Man Creates His Own Misery
Misuse of the Word / Voice

Holy - Holy is THE WORD - Which goes forth from out this Temple - For It is perfect in Its Concept - perfect in Its Completion -- And at no time shall It be made void -- For It is of the Light -- And It is of THE ESSENCE OF ALL THAT IS -- LIGHT! The Substance of ALL which IS -- And That Light is the first and LAST! - and nothing shall defile IT - or contaminate -- For IT is the ETERNAL SUBSTANCE from Which ALL things come into Manifestation -- I say - It is likened unto the ETERNAL - for It hast NO END/ NO BEGINNING -- IT IS -- It goes not - neither comes. -- IT IS! -- IT is EVER PRESENT -- IT is the SUBSTANCE from out which the rose is born/ from out which the Gods are fashioned --

IT is the Mighty Oak/ the stone/ the spider/ the web-- And too - It is the lowly poison which torments them which dare touch -- I say Light permeates "ALL" which hast form - in the world of form -- For thou livest in the "World of form" - and by the forms dost thou identify them -- Yet ye see not the Light from whence the Manifestation -- It is given unto thee to name the forms - one by one - and to study them - as though they were the Cause of the WORD ---

While I say unto thee - the "WORD" is the Cause of the forms -- The forms often torment them which have brought into being such forms - which turn against the ones which have brought them forth -- For it is said: "There is POWER in THE WORD" -- THE WORD which goes forth from out thine mouth hast Power to <u>give</u>/ to <u>take</u> - and to give comfort -- At no time shall It be used for the suffering of thine fellow men -- I say: thine fellow men shall learn well the folly of their misused energy -- For it is A POWER misused - wherein they find their own distorted creation which torments them -- Let no word pass thine lip - which would bring back unto thee the torment - which is so prevalent amongst mankind -- The MISUSED ENERGY is but the Cause of MANS SUFFERING -- So let it END!

I Am Come that they might Know wherein their strength lies -- So be it -

I AM the Lord thy God

Sananda

Recorded by Sister Thedra of the Emerald Cross

Let Us Speak of Peace

For this day - let Us speak of Peace --

For this let us become Peaceful - filled with Peace -- Let it be as NONE Known before -- Let it be OURS - wherein no man might be unto Us the purveyor of misfortune -- Let Us KNOW wherein We are staid – For this is it given unto Me to give unto thee - that which thou hast received of Me ---

For this is it given - that ye might drink from Mine Chalice - from Mine Cup -- Wherein ye might share with me that which the Father hast willed unto Me -- Be ye at Peace -- Let Peace fill thine heart ---

Rest in Me - and be ye not disturbed -- Let not thine heart be troubled -- For I say - ALL IS WELL -- ALL IS WELL WITH THEE Fear not -- For I say unto thee: COME - abide with Me - and I shall reveal unto thee many things. ---

Let it BE - As the Father hast Willed it --

I AM Sananda

Recorded by Sister Thedra of the Emerald Cross

The Black Magicians

Beloved Ones -- Hast thou not asked for Light? -- Wherein hast it been denied thee? Wherein hast it been denied one which hast asked for Light? ---

I say unto thee - there is none save thine own self which can close it out - save the self -- For no man hast the power to deny another -- There is none with such power -- It is given unto every man to search- and to find his own way -- It is given unto every man to search - and to find that for which he searches -- While I say - they which search for Light shall find -- They which seek signs and wonders shall find these. For there are ones which create their own signs and wonders - that they hold their fellows in subjection -- I say - they create the signs and wonders which hold their subjects in wonderment - that they might think them wise - that they might <u>appear</u> <u>Great</u>!

Lo it is as of old -- The Magician hast always flourished - while they stand in wonderment ---

I say unto them - their days shall be shortened- and they shall no longer bind the unknowing ones with their magic -- So be it I say: Seek ye Truth and Justice -- Seek ye the Light - and no magician shall delude thee -- Be ye as Ones responsible for thine misused energy - and it shall behoove thee to be alert -- For the Magicians flourish for their unknowing - for the ones they are wont to subject unto their way -- Be ye alert! ---

So be it I bid thee COME OUT from amongst them - and give of thineself that ye be lifted up ---

So be it I AM the Lord thy God

Sananda

Recorded by Sister Thedra of the Emerald Cross

Thine Time is Not Spent in the Frail Bodies

Behold ye this day - the Hand Work of THE LORD THY GOD! SEE IT -- KNOW ye that IT moves -- KNOW YE that the Hand moveth - and NO MAN can stay it -- It is the Hand of God that KEEPETH THEE, IT IS THE HAND OF GOD THAT HOLDETH THEE FAST -- For thou ART STAID IN HIM -- Thou ART NOT ALONE -- For this hast the WORD GONE OUT - "BE YE AS ONES PREPARED FOR THE GREATER PART" -- For there IS MORE -- Thine time is not spent within the frail/ puny bodies of flesh -- Thou art <u>not</u> of <u>flesh</u> - Thou art ETERNAL BEINGS -- Thou art not of Earth -- Thou art of the ETERNAL VARIETY - No man shall deny thee thine Inheritance -- It is thine BY DIVINE RIGHT -- So be it and Selah ---

I speak unto thee that ye might KNOW wherein thou art staid -- So let it BE ---

I AM Sananda

Recorded by Sister Thedra of the Emerald Cross

The Door

Mine Blessed Children -- This day let it be Known - that which I say unto thee -- Let it be KNOWN that I have said - lo many times: "I Am Come that they might KNOW themself to be as the Sons of God" -- "I Am Come that they MIGHT behold the Light - The Light Which lighteth every man which cometh into manifestation" -- I say I Am the Life - The Way -- I Am the DOOR through which they enter into the Holy of Holies -- For none return unto THE FATHER SAVE BY ME for I AM the DOOR-- I AM the LIGHT Which lighteth the WAY -- So be it that there is but ONE LIGHT - The ONE over ALL -- The ONE Which IS ALL - The ALL IN ALL ---

So be it that I Am ONE WITH THE ALL - The WHOLE-- For this is it given unto Me to KNOW that which lies ahead of thee -- I have gone before thee - that the Way be made straight - that ye might not fall that ye might follow in Mine Footsteps -- So be it that I give unto thee a Hand - and I bless thee this day -- Let them which have the mind to follow Me - Come - and I shall lead them - and I shall direct them in the Way in which they should go -- Ask of no man the Way - for they too come under the Law -- Ask of THE FATHER Which hast SENT ME - and I shall give unto thee as thou <u>art</u> <u>prepared</u> to receive -- So be it and Selah ---

I AM Sananda

Recorded by Sister Thedra of the Emerald Cross

Slowly But Surely Dost the Plan Unfold

Beloved Ones -- Thine hands shall be Mine Hands - thine time Mine time - for none other dost thou have -- Now it is come when the Part which shall be given unto thee to do - shall differ from that which hast been done -- YET - I say unto thee - the OTHER PART shall be finished ere thou movest into the Part which I have for thee -- Hold thine head high/ thine hand extended unto Me that I fill it -- Forget NOT that I Am the filler of THE HAND -- I AM the GIVER --

I AM THE TAKER -- I Am the Director of this ACTIVITY -- And I Am alert to ALL the ACTIVITY which IS OR SHALL BE -- I Am the OVERSEER - I Am not in lethargy -- Be ye as ones prepared for that which I shall give unto thee to do -- While it behooves Me to give unto thee ALL that is necessary unto thine part - it behooves thee to carry forth the Plan - which is given unto thee in its unfoldment -- For PART at a time it is given - and no small part dost thou have -- Discount it not! -- For there is a PLAN - and a PURPOSE within the unfoldment -- Slowly but surely dost the Plan unfold -- I say unto thee - Surely but slowly - the PLAN unfolds before thee -- Trip not thineself for thine unknowing-- Hasten ye to prepare thineself for the new Part - for it is surely and swiftly prepared for thee -- Let it BE - and be ye AT PEACE ---

Love ye one another -- Ask of the Father that He give unto thee thine Inheritance in full ---

Be ye blest this day - and I shall give of Mineself that it be so --

So let it BE --

I AM Sananda

Recorded by Sister Thedra of the Emerald Cross

I Keep Watch Over Mine Flock

Beloved -- It is given unto Me to see that which goes on within the hours of their sleep -- They know not that I Am He Which keeps watch over Mine Flock -- I say unto thee - I KEEP WATCH over MINE FLOCK – I Am alert -- I deprive not One of their lessons -- I say - none are deprived their lessons -- And it is given unto them to have many - and varied art they -- They are MANY! and VARIED INDEED! ---

Let it be said that none shall hide from Me - for I Am the Lord thy God - and I KNOW that which is hidden from them which have not yet attained unto the heights -- So be it that I shall lead thee gently - and I shall counsel thee in the Way of the Wise -- And I shall give unto thee the KEYS - and the DOOR shall swing wide before thee -- So be it - I AM THE DOOR - the DOOR through which ye enter into THE HOLY OF HOLIES ---

So be it I AM the Lord thy God -

Sananda

Recorded by Sister Thedra of the Emerald Cross

Be at Peace & Poise & I Shall Touch Thee

Beloved Ones -- With this Word I bless thee this day-- Let it bring unto All Great Peace -- And let it be unto thee the food and drink which shall suffice thee-- Let it bring unto thee the KNOWING that I Am with thee- that thou ART NOT ALONE ---

Give unto them this WORD - that they might know that which I say unto thee ---

Be ye as One blest for the Service unto "them"---

Hasten ye to do that which is given unto thee to do - and be ye not fearful for the doing -- Be ye as Ones prepared by the doing -- For this art thou prepared for Greater Service ---

They ask of thee: "What can I do to be prepared" I say unto them - be ye as ones responsible for All thine part/ all thine way/ all thine words/ deeds/ all the energy which is allotted unto thee -- Use it that the Father be <u>glorified</u> -- And let not the world of men beset thee --

ESTABLISH PEACE WITHIN THINESELF - that others might SEE - and Know that Peace is found within the world of men -- That they might know that thou hast touched the Hem of MINE GARMENT -- So be it that "they" seek Peace - knowing NOT where to find it-- Let thine heart be filled to the BRIM - that it might not be shaken -- Let them touch the Hem of <u>thine</u> <u>Garment</u> - and let it profit them ---

Be ye as the Chalice which I shall fill - and ye shall give unto others as I have given unto thee-- So be it that I Am the Lord thy God - and I Am The ONE which is SENT that ye night KNOW that there IS A PLAN - A DIVINE PLAN - Which goes NOT ASTRAY -- For that matter - none shall set it aside - for it is THE WILL OF MINE FATHER WHICH HAST SENT ME ---

Be ye at Peace and Poise - and I shall touch thee - and I shall give unto thee in <u>abundance</u> - that which I have kept for thee - for this day - For THERE IS A PLAN - and a time of fulfillment -- So be it MINE TIME I COME -- So be ye One with Me - and I shall be unto thee ALL that ye shall have need of ---

I AM Sananda

Recorded By Sister Thedra of the Emerald Cross

I Shall Give unto Thee Another Gift

HOLY - HOLY - O MINE SONS -- HOLY is the WORD of The Lord thy God - for HE hast spoken unto thee - that which shall be unto thee both food and drink -- It shall fill thine every need - and It shall replenish thee -- It shall be unto thee ALL which thou shall need -- For

IT is HOLY -- The Law IS THE LAW -- IT is given unto thee - that ye might KNOW wherein thine POWER Lies - wherein thine Strength lies.

I say unto thee: Thine Strength is MINE STRENGTH- for I give of MINESELF that ye be lifted up -- Cling not unto the puny fragments which bind thee - I say SOAR WITH ME unto the Heights - unknown to man -- For I KNOW NO LIMITATION -- I bid thee COME! Soar with ME - I shall take thee unto Mine Bosom - and bring thee into the Place of Mine Abode - that ye might ABIDE with ME forevermore -- So be it and Selah ---

I shall bless thee as NEVER BEFORE - for thou hast heard Me - and responded unto Mine Voice -- Thou hast responded unto Mine Touch -- For this shall I give unto thee Another Gift -- Praise ye the NAME of THE FATHER Which hast SENT ME ---

I AM Sananda

Recorded by Sister Thedra of the Emerald Cross

Sanat Kumaras Instructions to the Candidate

Beloved Ones -- There is but ONE LORD GOD -- That is THE ONE KNOWN AS SANANDA -- And too - let it be said that He hast set up this Temple - and BY HIS GRACE SHALL IT BE MAINTAINED -- It shall NOT BE PUT DOWN -- For it is given unto HIM to be the POWER by which it shall exist -- It shall exist for ALL TIME - for it is HIS - and HE hast the POWER and the Authority to maintain it -- HE hast the AUTHORITY AND THE POWER to Create that which is necessary unto its maintenance -- HE has the POWER WITHIN HIS HAND - and the Authority hast been given unto Him of THE FATHER Which hast SENT HIM -- So be it that the ONE Which hast been blest to give of Himself is THE LORD GOD - And HE is NO LESS for HIS GIVING - for His Power diminishes NOT for the giving ---

It is said: "By thine Service into the Light - do ye earn thine Passport into HIS ABIDING PLACE ---

So let thine Service unto the PLAN/ the LIGHT be for the Joy of Serving - that ALL men be lifted up-- So be it that I COME - EVEN AS HE - THE LORD GOD - that it BE -- Let it BE SO with thee -- Serve with a Glad Heart -- Be ye at Peace - and rest in the KNOWING that HE is COME that PEACE might be established WITHIN THEE.

So be it I AM -

Sanat Kumara

Recorded by Sister Thedra of the Emerald Cross

I See

Beloved Ones -- Upon Mine High Holy Mountain I stand - and I SEE them crying as ones beaten - beaten unto their knees -- I see them down trodden/ sick of heart/ heads bowed/ lamenting their lot -- I see them crucifying their fellow men -- I see them following after strange gods - seeking signs and wonders ---

I see them seeking afar for the Light -- I see them walking barefoot that they might atone their "evil ways" -- I see them giving alms that they might gain favor with ME - The Lord thy God! -- I see them paying homage to them which sit in high places - them which speak with many tongues -- I see them which serve many nations/ each unto his own part/ each unto the best of his ability -- I see them go and come -- I know that which prompts their coming and going ---

For I am not asleep -- I AM THE ONE SENT OF MINE FATHER that there BE LIGHT ---

I KNOW that which goes on in the world of men-- I give not of Mineself unto the unjust -- I Am not come that they be strengthened -- I Come that I might find MINE OWN - that they be gathered up/ that they be spared the death which is the end -- I say unto them which are of Mine Fold - COME! - COME YE - follow ye ME -

And I shall lead thee out of bondage ---

Be ye forever Blest --

I AM Sananda

Recorded by Sister Thedra of the Emerald Cross

Hidden Pearls

Beloved Ones -- This is the time of Great Learning - Great Revelation and Mighty shall it be --For I Am now prepared to make it KNOWN that I AM COME into the world of flesh - for the purpose of fulfilling the PLAN -- It is the purpose of Mine Coming/ of Mine speaking ---

For this do I say unto thee: "Hear ye that which I say unto thee -- Lift up thine eyes and BEHOLD that which I shall do" -- For art thou too not come - that this be done? -- Hast it not been given unto thee to be given a part? -- And art thou not Part of the PLAN?/ The Brotherhood? -- Art thou not given a Part - that which thou came to do?

Let it be said: that thine part is no small part! -- I say unto thee - thou ART ONE of MINE PLOWMEN -- Thou art the KEEPER of Mine Sobrieties -- Mine Words hast been given unto thee - that others might know that which I have said ---

These Mine Words shall be as the "Pearls" buried for a time -- Yet they shall be brought out - in ALL THEIR GLEAMING PURITY - and exposed unto ALL which have the eyes to see -- These WORDS shall be forever Sacred - for I have MADE THEM SO -- So let it be that they which seek - shall find -- For they shall <u>Serve Well Their Purpose</u> ---

So be it I have COME that there BE LIGHT --

I AM Sananda

Recorded by Sister Thedra of the Emerald Cross

There is a Beauteous Plan

Beloved Ones -- There is a Beauteous Plan - a Plan far Greater than that which man hast dreamed of - for it is THE PERFECT PLAN/

unlike man's design/ unlike man hast fashioned -- In his waiting - he hast blundered - and tripped himself up -- For that matter - he hast stumbled and fell many times -- Yet it is given unto him to lift himself up - and find his way ---

He hast but to follow where I lead him - for I Am The Lord of Lords The Host of Hosts - and I say unto thee: - Man shall become of the age of accountability - wherein he shall be self-responsible -- He shall be trustworthy - and THEN - he shall be given the fullness of the Great Plan - which is now unfolding before thee ---

So be it that there IS A MIGHTY PLAN! -- And it behooves thee to SEE it -- Yet for this hast thou waited - for thou seest in part only -- So be it I shall point the way - and ye shall follow after Me - and I shall lead thee into the Place wherein ALL things are KNOWN -- So let it be - as The Father hast willed it ---

I ask of thee: Follow ye ME - and I shall reveal many things unto thee ---

So be it - I AM Sananda

Recorded by Sister Thedra of the Emerald Cross

The Body of Christ
Spirit / Fear / Anxiety

Hast it not been said many times: "Thou art Mine hand and foot" -- And the part which I have given unto thee to do - is the Part for Mine Hand and Mine foot -- Yet I say unto thee: Come! Come up Higher - and be ye as the Head -- Be ye as ONE with ME -- Be ye as the <u>Head</u> - for I Am the Head -- I stand on Mine High Holy Mountain - and I SEE - and I KNOW that which Mine Feet do -- I KNOW wherein they stand -- I KNOW wherein they are made steadfast/ wherein their strength lies -- I Know wherein Mine Hand is staid -- I Know from whence Mine Strength cometh -- And at no time am I deceived - for I KNOW that which I AM - and wherein I Am staid ---

Let it be given unto thee - that ye KNOW even as I -- For this do I counsel thee by day and by night-- For I know no night - neither do I sleep -- I say: "I SLEEP NOT" -- Yet I say unto thee: "The Spirit sleepeth NOT" - neither is It troubled for the ways of man -- It is FREE from ALL FEAR/ ANXIETY -- It is aware-- Be ye as One which KNOWS - and be ye as Ones free from ALL anxiety and fear ---

KNOW YE that I Am with thee - and be ye as Ones prepared to give of thineself - that others be blest of Me - through thee - even as I bless thee -- So be it that I have spoken - and thou hast heard ME ---

I AM The Lord thy God

Sananda

Recorded by Sister Thedra of the Emerald Cross

Consciousness - Thinkers

Beloved Ones -- I speak this day on the subject of "Consciousness" - that which is the Comprehension of that which "IS" -- The consciousness is but the comprehension of that which IS -- It is the

KNOWING - of which WE speak -- The WORD is oft times misunderstood -- For it is NOT the play on words <u>only</u> -- It is the FULL COMPREHENSION OF BEING -- The fullness of that WHICH IS -- And wherein there is Light - there is KNOWING -- For ALL that there is - is contained within the LIGHT --

Yet for that matter - it matters not when it is not known - or comprehended -- For the darkness comprehends not the Light -- Yet THE LIGHT IS - and It is diminished not for the <u>unknowing</u> - for the <u>un</u> knowing - or the LACK of comprehension -- It IS - and for that I say: SEE - BEHOLD that WHICH IS - and be not deceived by the darkness -- For the ones in darkness but THINK! -- They are THE THINKERS!

THEY KNOW NOT! I say unto them - there are none so foolish - as the ones which THINK themself WISE ---

SO BE IT A TRUTH --

I AM Sananda

Recorded by Sister Thedra of the Emerald Cross

Extricated from 'The Web'

Beloved of Mine Being -- It is given unto Me to say unto thee: I Am the "MOST WORTHY GRAND MASTER" within the Inner Temple - and it behooves Me to give unto thee this Word -- And it shall be given unto them which ask for it - them which have given of themself - that they might be prepared to receive it ---

Let it BE KNOWN that THERE IS A PLAN - whereby they might be extricated from THE WEB which hast bound them -- It is the bounds which hast bound them unto the wheel of rebirth - within flesh! -- I say flesh is not the end - neither is it the Ultimate -- I say it is NOT THE END! for there are yet worlds untold - beyond thine imagination! - Worlds without end! - wherein ye shall walk in bodies of PURE LIGHT SUBSTANCE- wherein ye shall have no need for such gross and heavy/ clumsy -bodies as thine flesh body - which now hangs heavily/ densely UPON THEE ---

I say it is given unto Me to KNOW - for I have been within the place wherein I AM for a long period of time - wherein I KNOW the going in - and the going out – While I say - MANY TIMES have they taken unto themself the body of flesh -- I say it is now come when they shall be as ones eliberated from the Web -- It is come when they shall be given assistance -- Yet they shall CHOOSE the assistance offered by the MIGHTY COUNCIL - Which now STANDS BY TO ASSIST.

When they are of a mind to OBEY ALL THE LAWS - to give of themself - SELFLESSLY - that ALL men be given <u>as</u> they would be given -- When they ask nought of any man - for SELF - THEN WE take notice of them - and give of Ourself that they too be lifted -- So be it that they are wont to be lifted up - yet they are prone to give unto others the bitter cup -- Let it be the "First Principle" which motivates their every ACT/ <u>thought</u> - that of LOVE - of THE FATHER - THE SON - THE HOLY SPIRIT - which shall fill their CUP to overflowing- and THEN - by their Light We shall find them ---

So be it I have spoken - and thou hast heard Me--

I AM COME that ye hear --

I AM Sanat Kumara

Recorded by Sister Thedra of the Emerald Cross

The Father Speaks

Holy - Holy O Mine Sons -- Holy ART THOU – HOLY I SAY -- Be ye as Ones prepared to stand with ME – and SEE wherein thou hast been -- KNOW ye that The Way is opened before thee - That ALL IS WELL - WITH THEE--

For this have I spoken unto thee -- Let it be as thou hast prepared thineself -- I say - it is WELL -- While thou seest not the end of thine sojourn within bondage - it is nigh unto the end -- Wait upon ME - and be ye as Ones prepared for The Greater Part -- I say the "GREATER PART" is thine Eternal Inheritance-- Thou hast become NO LESS for having gone into bondage--

So be it I shall give unto thee that which I have kept for thee -- So be it - it is a Princely Fortune-- Be ye at Peace -- PEACE - MINE PEACE I give unto thee

For I AM thine FATHER ETERNAL -

Solen Aum Solen

Recorded by Sister Thedra of the Emerald Cross

SHE - THE LIONESS

Beloved Ones -- The time now approaches - when the Lion shall be loosed - and the dogs shall chase it as the rabbit -- And it shall find refuge in the place <u>wherein</u> <u>thou</u> <u>abideth</u> -- And at no time shall She - the Lioness overcome thee -- For it shall be given unto Her to weaken from Her Great Stress – She shall lie down at thine door - and pant for breath -- For She shall be with young - and Her strength shall be spent within the time which it takes to bring it forth ---

I say - She shall be as the one spent - for She shall be as one tossed before a Mighty Storm -- And She shall find refuge within thine Arms So be it She shall have no other place for shelter and Comfort---

Yet there shall be NO COMFORT in Her refuge ---

So be it I have spoken - and thou hast heard Me --

I AM Sananda

Recorded by Sister Thedra of the Emerald Cross

Great Gleamings
Word Trap

Beloved Ones -- The day brings forth Great Gleamings - and Great Revelations -- Let the Light go before thee-- WATCH - SEE - KNOW Walk ye with steps sure - for I Am thine forerunner -- I have gone before thee to prepare the way before thee - and at no time shall I forsake thee -- Hear ye that which I say unto thee -- Bring thine Self unto the Place which I have prepared for thee -- For by the obedience shall ye purchase thine own passport -- I say: By thine <u>obedience</u> unto the LAW - shall ye EARN thine passport into the Place of MINE ABODE ---

Wherein is it said: "As thou art prepared - so shall ye receive?" It is THE LAW! -- So shall it behoove thee to stand firm - and be ye at Peace -- Peace- MINE PEACE I give unto thee -- Fret not for thine unknowing - for I Am COME that ye MIGHT KNOW -- I have said unto thee many times - obey the LAW - and I shall TOUCH THEE - and ye shall be blest - even as I have been blest of Mine Father which hast SENT ME! ---

So be it I see them bowing down - and paying homage unto their "Strange gods" which would hold them in bondage -- They make for themself a wedge - that the forces of dark might use -- And for this do I say unto them: "I Am the Lord thy God - come to deliver thee -- COME follow ye ME" -- And for this do I say unto them: I Am sufficient unto thee - for Mine Father hast Sent Me -- I come not to give unto thee lengthy sermons/ the flowery words - which would be unto thee A "WORD TRAP" --

I say it is with GREAT KNOWLEGE of thine weakness - that I give unto thee the "WORD" of GOD - in its simplicity -- Strength shall be thine - for the "WORD" hast gone out Mine Mouth PERFECT - and IT is recorded for the GOOD of ALL men everywhere -- All which have a mind to receive it -- To the Ones which DO receive it - I say unto them: "Come follow ye Me - Be ye as One blest - and I shall give unto thee as I have received" -- So let it be. Wait upon Me - and I shall reward thee openly -- So be it I Am He which is SENT that the LAW be fulfilled - that MINE COVENANT be fulfilled - that I might do MINE PART -- So be ye as Ones responsible for thine Part -- I have spoken and I have been heard -- Now I say unto thee - PEACE - PEACE - MINE PEACE I GIVE UNTO THEE ---

I AM Sananda

Recorded by Sister Thedra of the Emerald Cross

A New Generation - A New People

Beloved Ones -- One in Me art thou - for thou ART NOT separate from ME -- For I AM THE LORD THY GOD - and for ME thou art sustained Thou art <u>kept</u> for this day - for I give of Mine Strength/ Mine POWER Which is invested within ME of Mine Father - Which hast SENT ME So be it - it is for ME that thou ART SUSTAINED---

Let it be understood that I - The Lord thy God AM NOT AFAR OFF --- I Am not to be put into a corner -- I Am at no time to be denied for I shall have Mine DAY -- MINE TIME IS COME - and I shall walk amongst thee as "THE ONE SENT" - for I AM HE! - I AM HE!! - I say unto thee - I AM HE!!! Which is SENT that there BE LIGHT - within the world of men -- So be it and Selah ---

I Am He Which hast always been the Lord of Hosts- I Am fortuned that PART -- So be it that I Am the Lord of Old -- I have <u>been</u> <u>no</u> <u>less</u> I shall be no less for having gone from thee for a time - wherein I closed the door behind Me - that man <u>see</u> <u>not</u> where I went -- I say man hast WAITED - that they be prepared to enter into MINE PLACE OF ABODE - for there is a Season unto all things -- ALL THINGS have their season -- Yet it is NOW the SEASON of GATHERING UP/ CLEANING -- Likewise it is the time of SOWING - for yet another Day -- And the fields shall be as prepared to receive the SEED for THE NEW DAY-- Let it be said that a NEW PEOPLE - A NEW GENERATION shall be raised up --

And that Generation shall be as none thou hast KNOWN -- For it shall be as one prepared to serve the LIGHT - and it shall be as The - and at no time shall it be as the present people/ the present generation - for it shall be the LIGHT -- It shall be the Physical Manifestation of THE LIGHT -- And this People shall come into manifestation through the manifestation of THE SPOKEN WORD -- This People shall NOT be the product of mans seed - for there shall be none -- I say - man shall not spawn this People of which I speak -- So be it I shall speak again of this Generation - this People ---

So be it - I Am prepared to Speak - for

I KNOW WHEREOF I SPEAK ---

I AM THE LORD THY GOD

Recorded by Sister Thedra of the Emerald Cross

Fearful of That Which They Know Not

Beloved Ones -- This day I say unto thee: Behold the Glory of the Lord Hold up thine head - and SEE that which He shall do -- For I say unto thee - The Glory of the Lord shall surpass ALL that man hast accomplished -- It shall be as nothing man hast seen-- For I say unto thee - this is the AGE OF LIGHT - when the Light shall go forth into every corner of the Earth -- And it shall not be withheld from them which seek the Light -- For it is now come when Great Changes shall come about - and many shall go into realms unknown unto them -- Some shall go prepared - yet others shall sleep long --

And these shall be as ones which have not alerted themself - within the realm of flesh-It is for this that WE of the MIGHTY COUNCIL say: Alert thineself - AWAKEN! ARISE! "Come follow ye Me" Yet they hear not -- For they seek not the Light -- There are many which seek the Light - Which I Am -- Yet they are fearful of that which they KNOW NOT -- Yet they give power unto strange gods in their unknowing -- They are deceived by the strange gods - which would hold them bound ---

Let it be said that there is nothing to fear - save thine own wonton/ thine own mind -- I say - let the mind which is MINE be the MIND which IS THINE -- So be it I AM COME that ye KNOW as I KNOW. For this AM I SENT of MINE FATHER ---

So be it I Am the Lord thy God

Sananda

Recorded by Sister Thedra of the Emerald Cross

Eternal Life

Mine Children -- There is nothing within the KINGDOM of MAN - which would equal the <u>Bright</u> and <u>Glorious</u> <u>Light</u> of the worlds yet uncreated - yet unmanifest -- For each and every world yet unmanifested - is within the Light of God the Father -- The Light Which IS - and ALWAYS SHALL BE - contains the THOUGHTS of the ALL WISE - ALL POWERFUL FATHER -- For HE hast placed HIS SEAL upon HIS CREATION - and closed it up for ALL TIME -- For HE is a fulfilled GOD -- ALL things are finished - Within HIM - there is NO TIME/ NO going/ NO coming -- Just the ETERNAL NOW! Just the BEINGNESS/ the EVERNESS ---

The going and the coming which man knows is but the pulsations of HIS HEARTBEAT-- As the flick of an eyelid - is thine eternity with HIM ---

Many times hast thou taken upon thineself - garments of flesh -- Through the Cosmos - thou hast traveled -- Forms and forms hast thou had - like unto none thou hast remembered ---

Myriad of forms hast thou had - or - taken unto thineself - that ye might be as One fulfilled! -- I say - that ye might experience ALL THINGS ---

Such is the WAY - and the LIFE Which I AM ---

I say unto thee - I AM the LORD thy GOD - and thou ART ONE WITH ME -- So be it I AM COME that ye might KNOW as I KNOW Be ye at PEACE and I shall Abide with thee ---

So be it I AM

Sananda

Recorded by Sister Thedra of the Emerald Cross

The Church Which the Lord God Hast Established

Beloved One -- The Time is now come when I shall speak out - and it shall be given unto me to KNOW whereof I speak -- For the Way is now open - and I shall enter into the affairs of men - and I shall set straight "Mine Church" -- And I shall make straight that which hast been made crooked -- I shall set Mine foot against the door thereof - and I shall not allow the traitors and the bigots to enter therein - for they have defiled the TEMPLE -- They have sold their passport for a poor penny - and at no time shall they enter herein without Mine notice/ without the preparation so necessary -- So be it that I Am aware of them and that which they do!

I Am not asleep --

I say unto thee: - These which are of Mine Flock shall be gathered up - and they shall be as ones prepared -- They shall be as ones WHICH HAVE GONE THE LAST MILE WITH ME -- And these shall KNOW ME - and they shall be as the Church which I the Lord God hast established-- They shall KEEP THE LAW -- They shall abide by the LAW which I bring - and they shall be as the "Sons of God" - for these have kept their Covenant with Me ---

While it is given unto SOME of them to wait for the season of gathering - I say their waiting shall be cut short -- For I the Lord God shall cut short the season of waiting -- For I have given unto them a New Dispensation - and I Am come that THIS DAY bring forth GREAT FRUIT! - which shall be unlike any man hast known -- I say unto them which have followed the magicians - they have seen nothing which shall compare unto the Glory of God The Father ---

He - The Father hast sent Me that the Children of the Earth be given as they are able to comprehend - as they are prepared to receive -- I say: they shall be plucked from out the prisons/ out of the pit/ from out the dens of the dragon -- These which have lost their way - yet these shall be of a mind to follow where I lead them -- They shall KNOW ME -- They shall KNOW MINE VOICE - and follow as the Lambs know their Shepherd -- And for this Am I the Shepherd of Mine Flock -- I say unto thee: Mine Flock is scattered upon a thousand hills - yea - into a thousand valleys have they descended -- And at no time shall one be lost from Mine view/ from Mine sight - for I know them - and I am not of a mind to sacrifice ONE of Mine unto the forces of darkness -

YET:

I say_ it is not sufficient that they cry out for surcease - it is necessary that they learn well their lessons -- That they are now prepared to go the last mile with Me --

I say unto them which have heard Mine Voice - turn not from Me - for the end is in sight ---

I say unto them which have not heard Mine Voice- "AWAKEN YE! AND ARISE! -- Come follow ye ME - and I shall deliver thee out of bondage!" ---

Hear ye ME - for this have I COME ---

I AM the Lord God - Sent of THE FATHER--

So Be It I AM Sananda

Recorded by Sister Thedra of the Emerald Cross

To Them That Have Ears

Behold ye - The Hand Work of the Lord thy God -- See ye the Manifestation thereof -- The WILL OF THE FATHER SHALL BE DONE - throughout HIS KINGDOM -- HE hast sent many SONS forth that the LAW be fulfilled - that THE PLAN be fulfilled - that HIS WILL be done in the Earth---

I say unto them which are of the Earth: Concern not thineself with other worlds - until thou hast LOVED THE EARTH sufficiently to RESPECT and ABIDE BY HER LAWS-- For there is A LAW governing ALL REALMS -- Thereby ye shall be governed - while within that Realm -- I Say - while within each Realm thou comest under the LAW of that Realm -- And it is given unto ME to KNOW whereof I speak -- Feign not wisdom concerning these things - of which I speak for I say unto thee - ALL thine learning is not sufficient! ---

I Am come that ye might COME TO KNOW -- While it is said many times: "PREPARE THINESELF" ---

I say: When thou hast put aside all thine prejudices/ thine bigotry/ all thine preconceived ideas of ME and about ME -- When thou hast complied unto the LAW - I shall TOUCH THEE - and ye shall KNOW as I KNOW -- Be ye NOT deceived by their flowery sermons - and great and learned sermons -- For I say unto thee - I Am COME unto thee as One Simple/ ONE SENT OF MINE FATHER - that ye might be delivered from the enemies trap -- Let it be said - that the intellect of man hast deceived him -- That the "Whore rides high upon the shoulders of the Goat" -- Let it be said that the Goats shall be separated from the sheep ---

I say unto Mine Sheep: "Come follow ye where I lead thee - and I shall give unto thee Comprehension-- Wherein hast thou found Comprehension which I bring unto thee - save through ME - The Lord thy God? ---

I tell thee - there are ones which would be ensnared - by the whore for her beauty and charm alone --- Yet she is a treacherous charmer -- She hast the reins within her hands - that she might lead thee astray -- For her works are many - and they are as the tares within the wheat -- These shall be as the tares - and gathered into the flames - wherein they shall be burned - and be no more ---

I say - they shall be as nought against MINE '"WORD" - Which is given unto ME OF MINE FATHER -- So let it be said THIS DAY - that I AM COME to deliver up the Ones which are of a mind to follow ME.

None other do I call -- For none other hast the mind to follow ME. None other hast ears to hear---

I call unto the Ones which have the mind which is of ME -- For these shall be made to hear - and SEE-- For these are the Ones I AM SENT to bring out -- So be it that there are many NOW PREPARED to receive ME and of ME -- Yet others shall wait the season of awakening-- I shall awaken them in due season - when they have taken unto themself sufficient Strength - to move themself - under their own power/ Power of FREE WILL---

I speak unto them which have ears -- These shall hear that which I say ---

So be it I AM

Sananda

Recorded by Sister Thedra of the Emerald Cross

The Church Shall Be Set Aright

Beloved Ones -- The day draws near - when there shall be ONE from out the Inner Temple - REVEAL HIMSELF unto thee -- And it shall be for the GOOD of ALL -- And at no time shall ye be deceived by HIM -- I say unto thee This One was the CHOSEN for the PART Which He shall have - within this NEW DAY -- And it is fortuned unto Him to be as One in flesh - "In flesh" this day -- And for this shall He be as One prepared to do that which HE SHALL DO -- And it is given unto Him to be the One which hast COME that HIS PEOPLE be led aright- that THE CHURCH BE SET ARIGHT -- That the ones which have been misled - be led out of darkness -- That the Ones which are of HIS PEOPLE - might be delivered up -- Yet I say: It is for the GOOD OF ALL- that He hast taken upon Himself the GARMENT OF FLESH -- Yet flesh shall not bind Him -- He shall be FREE - that He go and come EVEN AS I -- I AM COME that All might be FREE -- Yet I bring NOT PEACE - I make way for PEACE---

SO LET IT BE --

I AM Sananda

Recorded by Sister Thedra of the Emerald Cross

To Mine Flock I Say

To "Mine Flock" I say: "Come - Come ye and follow ME" For <u>none</u> <u>other</u> do I accept -- They shall HEAR Mine Voice and come -- They shall be obedient unto THE CALL- for they shall KNOW Mine Voice and as I give of Mineself that ALL mankind be lifted up - I say unto them AWAKEN! and come forth -- Yet they which have not ears - shall NOT hear - for they are as ones deaf -- They are as ones which have not the mind to follow ME -- They are as ones blind - for they have their own hands before their eyes that they see not! -- They have not the WILL to follow Me / Go where I go ---

Yet -- I say: They shall be as ones prepared- that they be put into their own environment - wherein they shall await the time of ripening Then they shall come forth as the SEED from the POD -- Then they shall be as ones MATURE -- Then they shall be as ones prepared for the place wherein ALL THINGS are KNOWN -- So be ye at PEACE - and let them which have a WILL to follow ME come -- Them which are wont to follow strange gods - let them GO -- Be YE about the Father's Business - and heed the WORDS Which I have given unto thee -- So be it that I Am the Lord thy God - Sent of HIM that ye might KNOW - that ye be brought out of bondage -- For this have I said unto thee - PEACE - PEACE - PEACE -- I SAY PEACE -- And all which have the <u>Will</u> to accept the Peace which is Mine - shall drink of Mine Chalice - they shall drink and be filled -- They shall be satisfied -- Then they shall KNOW as I KNOW -- So be it that I have Spoken the WORD Let it fall where it will -- For I AM that I AM

Sananda

Recorded by Sister Thedra of the Emerald Cross

The New Nation

HOSANNAS unto GOD THE FATHER -- This day I say unto thee - let thine heart rejoice that THIS DAY is come - wherein thou shall be blest as in none other -- I say: Ye shall be blest THIS DAY as in none other - for THIS is the DAY for which thou hast waited -- So be it ye shall come forth as a PEOPLE - ONE: - ONE NATION - that of the NEW NATION -- And its name shall be called "WORLD" -- Yet it shall not be as the world which thou knowest This Day -- For it shall be as a NEW NATION - UNDIVIDED/ and UNSCATHED for the experience which it has had ---

For it shall lick its wounds - and heal them - and sit down at the Council table - and Counsel with ME -- And I shall lead them out of the Valley of the Shadows -- I say I shall counsel them - and they shall be as ones prepared to follow ME -- For this Am I SENT -- I say: It is now come when I have given forth a Fiat: "LET THERE BE UNITY AMONGST MINE PEOPLE" - and it shall BE -- For this have I divided them into twos and threes - and I shall give unto each as he is prepared to receive -- So be it I Am the Lord thy God - and I Am prepared for THIS DAY -- I say unto them which have EARS Hear ye - that which I say unto thee -- Unto them which have not the ear to hear - I AM COME!! AWAKEN YE! - And BE QUICKENED!!!

So be it - these shall await their time of quickening - for I Am in NO HURRY -- So be it I Am at Mine Post - prepared for THAT DAY when they are sufficiently MATURED -- Then - I shall pluck them as the pea from the pod ---

So let it be - the time / the place of Maturing --

And Come ye follow ME - and I shall lead thee Aright ---

I AM Sananda

> **Recorded by Sister Thedra of the Emerald Cross**

He Is the Root

Beloved Ones -- The day swiftly approaches - when there shall be a Great Light envelope the Earth - and it shall be as no other time -- When man shall come into the Knowledge of that which they are - they shall walk in this <u>Knowledge</u> -- And they shall not be boastful of that which they <u>are</u> - for they shall KNOW that they ARE - by the "GRACE" of Our Father - AMEN -- They He shall KNOW that they are not sufficient unto themself - that they are <u>not</u> a people separate from HIM.

They shall KNOW that HE IS THE ROOT - They are the SEED -- They ARE because HE IS -- And were it not SO - I would not tell thee So be it that man hast forgotten from whence he came -- He hast forgotten his inheritance -- Yet he shall be as one prepared for to receive it -- He shall wait for his day - when he hast properly prepared himself - for to receive his estate - WILLED unto him of the Father Eternal ---

He shall first be as one <u>willing</u> to be prepared -- He shall let the WILL Of The Father be done IN HIM - THRU HIM - BY HIM - AND FOR HIM -- THEN - he shall be as one obedient unto MINE VOICE - and I shall direct him into the Way in Which the Father would have him go -- For I AM "THE DIRECTOR" "THE WAYSHOWER" "THE LORD OF LORDS" "THE LORD OF HOSTS" -- I AM ALL these and more -- Yet I BOAST NOT of MINE PART -- For I Am SENT of MINE FATHER - that I might KEEP MINE COVENANT WITH HIM.

I say: I AM COME that - HIS WILL BE DONE ON EARTH - that THE KINGDOM be established upon the EARTH -- So let it BE as HE HAST WILLED IT ---

I speak unto ALL men everywhere - as The "ONE SENT"-- So let them which have ears - hear that which I say -- Let them do their Part - and I shall do Mine---

So be it I AM The Lord thy God

Sananda

Recorded by Sister Thedra of the Emerald Cross

To The Thinkers
Sananda

Beloved Ones - This day let it be recorded that which I say unto thee - It is Mine Part to give it unto them which are of a mind to receive it -- And It shall bless them which doth receive It -- So be it and Selah ---

There are a number of people upon the Earth - which doth consider themself "Christians" -- Let us consider the Law -- And is it not written that they which DARE call themself Christ-ians shall obey the Law? - I say unto thee - it is written - "they shall obey the Law" -- And it hast been given unto Me to see the poor in Spirit go about as ones puffed up passing judgement upon their Brothers which are of another Race/ another color/ another place/ <u>another</u> <u>opinion</u> ---

Yet they have the part of the hypocrite and blasphemer -- They are not abiding by the Law which is given unto them -- They are giving unto themself credit for being wise - and they seek not <u>their</u> <u>own</u> salvation through obedience unto the Law ---

I say they shall first be free from ALL bondage- then they may turn unto their Brother - that <u>He</u> be lifted up -- For there is not one which thinks himself wise - which hast been freed from all bondage -- They are as yet bound within the Earth - and the vehicles of flesh -- I tell thee these which do give unto themself credit for being wise - are the "poor in Spirit"-- They are the ones which set themself up and call themself "good" -- They are the ones which say "come follow ye me" -- Yet they know not whither THEY goest -- They are as the blind leading the blind therefore they fall into the pit -- Let it be said now - that they shall lift themself out by their own effort - for they alone are responsible for their fall! ---

<u>I</u> Come that there be Light! Yet they see not!

They look NOT for Light --

They have their own hands before their eyes - they see not that which is before them - they KNOW NOT -- These are the THINKERS!! ---

These are the ones which set themself up as paragons of Christianity - and they say - "follow ye me"---

This day I speak out against the hypocrites and the wrongdoers -- So let it be heard throughout the Land --

I AM Sananda

Recorded by Sister Thedra of the Emerald Cross

Not One Shall Stand Alone

Harken unto these Mine Words - and I shall give unto thee <u>greater capacity</u> for learning – For I have much to reveal unto thee -- I have said that I shall reveal many things unto thee - and have I not kept Mine Covenant with thee? -- Have I not given of Mineself that ye might have LIGHT? ---

I AM COME that it be so - So let it be - for the good of ALL MANKIND ---

Now it is given unto thee to be as Mine Servants - and there is not one which shall stand alone - for I have said: "I shall bind up Mine sheaves - as one bundle - and I shall separate the tares from the wheat" The tares shall be burned as the chaff - and the WHEAT I shall bring into MINE PLACE OF ABODE - and nothing shall despoil that which I bring into MINE PLACE - for I AM the Householder - and I Am a prudent One - given unto watchfulness -- And not one shall break through Mine fortress - and pilfer that which is MINE -- For I AM not asleep! -- I watch with diligence that which is MINE---

I say unto thee - BEHOLD THE WORK OF THE LORD THY GOD ---

I have spoken unto thee - for thou hast come that ye might hear that which I say unto thee ---

So let it BE - for this have I spoken--

Be ye AT PEACE --- Love ye one another - and I shall show unto thee GREAT AND WONDERFUL WORKS ---

So be it I AM

The Lord thy God

> **Recorded by Sister Thedra of the Emerald Cross**

The Earth Shall Have a New Port

Beloved of Mine Being -- Let it be said this day - that I Am the One sent that the Earth and the children thereof be lifted up -- I am come that the Earth be brought out - and delivered up - that the WHOLE of the MIGHTY GALAXY be blest - and that the Earth have a new port - wherein She shall be received with GREAT JOY and dignity -- That is fortuned unto ME to be the OVERLORD of that activity - for I am the ONE sent for that part ---

I Am the ONE which hast given unto the Earth of Mine STRENGTH - of MINE LOVE and assistance - that She be held upon Her COURSE - that the children of the Earth might not perish ---

NOW I say unto thee - it shall be given unto many to see the great change which shall come about within Her people -- For it is so said: "Change there shall be" - and let it be - for it is the WILL of THE

FATHER Which hast sent thee forth -- Have I not given of Mineself lo the eons of time - that it be spared-- For this do I now say unto thee - hold ye steadfast - for thou shall come into the NEW PLACE OF ABODE wherein ye shall stand as ones prepared to partake of OUR VICTORY - OF OUR FORTUNE - and such JOY "MAN" hast not known ---

Let it be said: "We shall rejoice together - we shall partake of the same cup" - and know that there is but ONE FATHER - MOTHER GOD - and WE are the FAMILY which HE HAST BROUGHT FORTH AS ONE - ONE IN HIM -- By HIM have WE been brought forth -- Now ye shall walk with firm steps -- Ye shall carry the ROD - and WEAR THE CROWN - and ye shall speak that which HE shall give unto thee to say -- Ye shall speak with authority and compassion for ye shall KNOW that which ye shall say ---

Ye shall be as the SON RETURNED from a long sojourn - and there shall be <u>great</u> <u>rejoicing</u> through ALL the Cosmos. Endless shall be the reverberation of the joyous anthems which shall ring out throughout the COSMOS ---

Let it BE -- For this have I revealed unto thee Mine part -- Behold the HAND OF GOD - SEE IT MOVE - for IT MOVETH SURELY AND SWIFTLY - AND MERCIFUL ---

I AM Sanat Kumara

Recorded by Sister Thedra of the Emerald Cross

Seek Ye First the Kingdom

Beloved Ones -- Children of Mine own Heart art thou - Children of Mine OWN IMAGING art thou - born from out MINE OWN BEING For I have breathed forth the Substance of Mineself - that ye might BE I have willed unto thee the fortune of SONS -- I have given unto thee the Inheritance which is befitting the SONS OF THE ETERNAL FATHER -- For I say unto thee - the PART which I have willed unto thee is not the Earthly supply - the poorer part -- For the ETERNAL PART is GREATER than ALL the fortunes of Earth OR the Heavens there about -- For this is it said: "Seek ye FIRST the KINGDOM of the heavens - the KINGDOM of GOD THE FATHER - and all else shall be added unto thee" ---

There is <u>nothing</u> to compare unto that which I have fortuned unto MINE SONS - which shall return unto ME unscathed - unharmed ---

Let thine eye be single - and rejoice this day that thou art within MINE EMBRACE -- That I shall give unto thee that which I have held intact for thee -- And it is but the "GREATER PART" -- Be ye as ones made "WHOLE" - as ones returned unto ME - as ONE WITH ME - and I shall array thee in the ROYAL RAIMENT - give unto thee the STAFF - "THE ROD OF POWER" - and I shall place upon thine head the CROWN which I have fashioned for thee -- And ye shall sit upon Mine right hand - and I shall proclaim thee "WHOLE" ---

<u>I</u> shall do this and more! for there is not words within thine vocabulary which can convey the GLORY of THINE INHERITANCE-- Thine fortune is vast beyond expression in any language -- Thus it is said: "Behold! the GLORY OF GOD THE FATHER!" -- "BEHOLD! THE GLORY OF THE LORD GOD!"- for

HE is the LORD OF LORDS - THE HOST OF HOSTS - and HE sits upon Mine right hand - and gives of HIMSELF that ye be lifted up -- So shall it BE - Let it BE -- For this hast HE been sent unto thee - that ye might come into MINE PLACE - which I have prepared for thee---

So be it I AM thine Father Eternal

Solen Aum Solen

Recorded by Sister Thedra of the Emerald Cross

There is but One Source

Beloved Children -- There is but ONE PARENT - ONE SOURCE - and from this SOURCE hast thou been sent forth - even as the branch of the tree -- Thou art NOT separate from thine SOURCE - thou art ONE WITH IT -- And thou art not lacking in Substance - for I AM the Substance ---

I AM the Source - I AM thine Source -- I say unto thee Mine children -

I AM the Source - I AM thine Father ---

I give unto thee that thou might be as ONE WITH ME - and thou art NOT apart from ME - and ye have NO OTHER Source - for I AM the Source ---

I AM THE SUBSTANCE

I AM the MANIFESTATION of the Substance --

I AM that which is MANIFEST --

I AM the UN-manifest --

I AM THE ALL - for there is

NO Substance other that the LIGHT which I AM ---

So be it I AM Solen Aum Solem – in which thou art ensouled --

I AM thine Father Eternal

Recorded by Sister Thedra

In Tongues

Beloved Ones -- Let it be recorded this day - that I the Lord thy God speaketh with the tongue of men - with the tongue of Angels - with the tongue of Silence -- With the tongue of fire do I speak -- Yea unto all men in his own tongue do I speak - that he might come to know that I AM the Lord God - the Lord of Hosts -- The Lord of Lords AM I ---

I seek Mine own - and I AM come that Mine own might know Me that I might reveal unto them that which hast been hidden up - that they might walk in darkness no more ---

I AM come that Mine own be brought out of bondage -- So be it that I AM the ONE sent that it be so---

Let it suffice thee that I AM HE - that it is now come when I shall walk with thee - and counsel thee - that ye might go where I go -- So be it that I bring with Me great LIGHT/ POWER - which is Mine by inheritance -- For all that Mine Father hast is Mine - for HE hast willed unto Me all that He hast -- So be it that I bid thee partake of <u>Mine</u> <u>Cup</u> Drink ye from Mine Chalice - and let US rejoice together -- So be it - it shall be as the Father hast willed it ---

Be ye blest of ME and by ME -- I AM HE which cometh after Mine Forerunner -- Receive him in Mine Name ---

I AM

Sananda

Recorded by Sister Thedra of the Emerald Cross

The Seamless Garment

Beloved Ones -- This day I say unto thee - thine time IS COME - when ye shall be given in <u>great</u> <u>measure</u> - and wherein ye shall know thine inheritance - wherein ye shall stand arrayed within the LIGHT - which shall be unto thee thine "Seamless Garment" -- And ye shall walk with surety and fall not -- For this have I revealed unto thee Mine precepts - I have given unto thee in great measure - yet I say unto thee - thine fortune is NOT spent -- I have kept for thee the GREATER PART -- So be it - it is a princely fortune indeed -- I have said unto thee - ye shall stand arrayed in the SEAMLESS GARMENT - not fashioned by man - and it is SO -- So shall it BE as The Father hast willed it -- <u>Let</u> <u>not</u> <u>thine</u> <u>foot</u> <u>slip</u> - for there is none so sad as the one which betrays his trust - for he but betrays himself -- So be it that I have extended Mine hand unto thee -- See it and know ye that I Am come that ye be lifted up -- So be it - I Am the ONE sent that ye be brought out of bondage - So be it I AM

The The Lord thy God

Sananda

Recorded by Sister Thedra of the Emerald Cross

They Shall

Be ye blest of Me and by Me -- For this do I speak unto thee -- Let it be said that I bless thee with Mine Presence - that I AM the Lord thy God - Come that ye be blest ---

Now - while it is time - let it be given unto thee to give unto them these Mine words - and it shall profit them to receive them (these Mine Words) -- For it is for their sake that I say unto thee - record that which I say unto thee - that they might know that which I say unto thee ---

They shall come into the fullness of their estate - when they have so prepared themself to receive it -- They shall first become of age - the age of <u>accountability</u> wherein they know - wherein they obey the Law Wherein they are self-responsible for their every act/ deed/ word -- And they shall bear the responsibility of their own burden -- Their own offal they shall transmute -- They shall purify themself - and be as ones filled with love for their own kind -- They shall seek the Light - and they shall find - for it shall not be hidden - and for that shall they seek - for unto them which seeketh it shall be revealed -- Seek ye the fullness of ME - and I shall reveal Mineself unto thee -- So be it -

I AM the Lord of Lords -

The Host of Hosts -

The Son of God -

Sananda

Recorded by Sister Thedra of the Emerald Cross

The Day of Fulfillment Is Come

Beloved Ones -- Thine hour hast come when ye shall be given in <u>greater measure</u> - and ye shall be as ones prepared -- Ye shall find within the WORD - the witness of thine part -- Ye shall know that the day of fulfillment <u>IS</u> COME - that the WORD is <u>surely</u> <u>fulfilled</u> - that I The Lord thy God have kept Mine COVENANT With thee ---

Ye shall know this - and more - for I shall open up Mine Store unto thee - and ye shall see that which is concealed therein -- <u>Then</u> ye shall know - and rejoice that THIS DAY is come - for <u>long</u> hast thou walked in bondage - one step at a time - seeing not the next -- NOW ye shall walk with surety - KNOWING where thou goest -- Ye shall know that thou art staid in ME - and ye shall falter not - neither shall ye turn thine face from ME any more -- No more shall ye go out -- So be it that I Am glad this day IS come - for long have I waited -- Now I Am the Host of Hosts - and I say unto thee - The Mighty Hosts rejoice in the <u>Victory</u> of one of Mine Own -- So be it We shall rejoice together -- Praise ye the NAME of Solen Aum Solen ---

Sananda hast spoken - and thou hast heard ME

I AM - that I AM

Recorded by Sister Thedra of the Emerald Cross

I Come That He Learn His Lessons

Behold in ME the LIGHT which I AM - and know ye that I AM the ONE sent that ye be lifted up -- Behold in thineself the Light which is the LIGHT of GOD The Father -- Behold in thineself the Light which is HIS - for He is the Source of ALL LIGHT -- He is THE LIGHT which is everpresent and omnipotent -- He is ALL that is LIGHT -- All else is of no consequence - for it hast NO reality - no root - no fortune within reality - for it is but of the mind of men - that it doth appear to be real --

I say - that which is not of LIGHT hast no reality - no Substance - for out of the LIGHT Substance cometh all things which are REAL - and of lasting substance -- All else shall pass away as the shadows - and be no more - for they are but illusions - created by MANS unknowing - "HIS THINKING" - and his thinking does not make of them (his illusions) real -- They shall torment him for a time - until he learns the true from the false -- So let him learn his lesson well So be it - I come that he learn of ME the true from the false -- So be it I deny him not his lessons -- So be it I set before him a table - and he shall choose that which he will ---

Yet I say unto him - be ye alert - watchful -- choose ye wisely - and know ye the true from the false -- I AM with thee --

So be it I shall bless thee according unto thine Service unto the LIGHT Which I AM.

Recorded by Sister Thedra of the Emerald Cross

In Knowing - We Rejoice

Beloved -- Say unto them in Mine Name - I AM COME -- I come that they might go where I go -- I come that they might know as I know -- I come that they be blest as I have been blest of Mine Father - even as I have been blest -- And I say it is for the GOOD of ALL that I come - Yet I come as a thief in the night -- When they are asleep I come! -- I come - I go - and some shall sleep still - knowing not that I AM - that which THEY are -- For that matter - I say unto thee - see and know - and be ye lifted up -- It shall be for thine <u>knowing</u> that ye shall be made to rejoice - not because of thine THINKING! ---

I say - I come that ye might KNOW - yet ye shall be as one willing to follow where I lead thee -- Yet they say - I know Him <u>not</u>! -- I say - be ye as ones prepared - THEN I shall reveal Mineself unto thee -- While they ask of strange and devious gods - I say unto them - be ye as ones prepared that I might come in and counsel thee - and I shall lead thee aright - that ye might HAVE Knowledge of Me -- Yet I tell thee - I do not reveal Mineself unto the unjust and the imprudent -- I give not Mine pearls unto babes - which would but throw them at the feet of their idols - where-upon they would be trodden -- I Say I Am not so foolish -- Let it suffice thee that I AM the Lord thy God - come that ALL men be lifted up --

I say - Let them which WILL- Come – and they shall hear - and know that which I sayeth ---

So be it I AM

Sananda

Recorded by Sister Thedra of the Emerald Cross

The Many Membered Body

Beloved Ones -- Mine hand I place upon thee - and I say unto thee: Thine hand is Mine hand - and thine voice is Mine Voice - and thine feet is Mine feet -- And I say unto thee - come unto Me and be ye as ones made whole - for thou art as ONE - and there is no separation from ME - for I AM the Lord thy God - and thou ART ONE WITH ME -- Therefore I speak unto thee as Mine own - for I have said unto thee - thou art "MEMBERS of MINE BODY" - and I Am speaking unto thee as such -- For I Am the HEAD of this BODY - "THE MANY MEMBERED BODY" --

While thou shall walk upon the Earth as ones in flesh and bone - forget not that I AM the ONE Which hast gone before thee - that ye too might follow in Mine footsteps -- For I have seen the part which thou now playeth - and I KNOW the <u>Whole</u> <u>Play</u> -I have not forgotten My lines - neither the scenes <u>I</u> have played -- While I say thou art now playing these scenes upon a darkened stage - yet the lights shall become brighter - so bright that it shall be blinding unto them which are not prepared to behold the GLORY of THE LORD -- I say I bring unto thee GREAT LIGHT - and thou shall behold it - and NOT fall upon thine face in blindness -- I say unto thee - lift up thine face - behold the LIGHT which I AM - and behold the LIGHT of the NEW DAWN which I bring -- Behold within thine Self the Light which lighteth EVERY MAN which is born of ME - for I AM The LORD thy GOD -

Sananda

Recorded by Sister Thedra of the Emerald Cross

I See Thine Victory as Won

Beloved Ones -- The time <u>swiftly</u> approaches when ye shall see that which hast been accomplished within thine sojourn -- And it is given unto Me to see and know -- I too know the end of thine journey - and the suffering - and the Victory! I see thine VICTORY as WON - and I see thine return as accomplished -- I know the fullness of thine accomplishment -- I AM THE VICTOR and I know the path of attainment - it is not attained without effort - great effort - sincerity of purpose -- GREAT and MIGHT Strength is given unto them with sincerity of purpose - and a WILL to attain the VICTORY -- I say unto thee: "Hail! Hail! unto the Victor - for he hast endured - he hast attained!!! -- At last he hast come into the place Mine Abode - wherein he might share with Me Mine fortune --

I tell thee of a surety - I share not Mine fortune with the laggards and the traitors -- Therefore I say unto thee - betray not thineself - turn not thine face from Me -- For it is given unto Me to know them - and I have given unto them sufficiently that they too might be preserved for the NEW DAY -- So be it I have brot forth many prophets - that they too be prepared - yet they ask not of Mine Prophets - they seek strange gods and counsel with the dead - that they might be justified in their opinions - and in their own ways -- They ask foolish questions of the dead!! - and they receive foolish answers - while I stand ready to lift them up and give unto them as I have received -- So be it that I have received Mine Inheritance in full.

So be it I speak unto them which have ears to hear -- <u>These</u> shall hear - and unto "These" I shall reveal Mine Precepts -- I shall open up Mine Storehouse unto them which follow in Mine footsteps - for these I shall reward openly --

I AM the Lord thy God

Recorded by Sister Thedra of The Emerald Cross

I Shall Anoint Thee with Oil

Beloved Ones -- This day let it be known that I the Lord thy God hast spoken - and thou hast heard Me -- Let all men know that which I say unto thee - that they might seek Me out - that they too might go where I go - that they too might be prepared to receive their inheritance ---

Now it is come when ye shall be given a greater work - and ye shall do that which I give unto thee to do with swiftness of tongue and foot. Ye shall be as ones which I shall anoint with "Oil" - and I shall give unto thee abundantly - that ye might have all that is necessary unto thine own attainment -- Yet as I give unto thee - ye shall give unto them which ASK of thee -- Ye shall be as ones supplied - that they too might be supplied -- And so be it that ye shall be fed from Mine own hand -

for I shall give unto thee Water which shall quench thine thirst - and the Bread which shall nourish thine body - for thine body shall be Mine body - and ye shall run and weary not -- Ye shall give of thineself that others be nourished - even as I nourish thee-- And ye shall be no less forgiving of thineself - for the oil shall not diminish - for I am the Oil with which I shall anoint thee -- Ye shall pass into the Place wherein I abide - and ye shall be as ones prepared - for I shall provide thee with thine passport - and no man shall keep thee out - for I am the Door Keeper and I am alert -- As the Door Keeper I bid thee enter in - into Mine abiding place ---

So be it I AM the Lord thy God

Sananda

Recorded by Sister Thedra of The Emerald Cross

The Key - Use It

Beloved Ones -- This day let it be recorded that I am come - that I am the One sent that ye might be brot out - that ye might abide with Me forevermore -- I tell thee of a certainty that I am come that ye might return unto thine rightful estate - that ye might have thine inheritance in full -- So be it I am HE which cometh into flesh that it be made pure that it be purified -- Yet flesh is not the fulfillment -- Flesh is FLESH and cometh under the law of flesh - thus it hath beginning and end -- While I am not flesh - neither am I of flesh - I can take upon Mineself the flesh -- While it binds Me not -- it serves Mine purpose for taking such a vehicle as flesh - for flesh comprehendeth flesh -- For that matter

I am the FIRST BORN - then it is given unto Me to take the form of flesh that "man" be lifted up -- And for that have I taken unto Mineself a body of flesh substance - "Pore" ---

While thou now hast the body of flesh - the substance of flesh shall be made better - for thou hast made it so -- So be it that I have given unto thee a KEY -- Take it and open up the Inner Door - and enter ye therein - for I bid thee enter in - into the INNER TEMPLE of The MOST HIGH LIVING GOD ---

So be it I bow before thee in Holy

Adoration of Mine Father's

Manifestation --

I AM Sananda

Recorded by Sister Thedra of The Emerald Cross

It Is Hallowed by the Word

Behold! Behold! For I say unto thee - Behold that which I shall do -- I say unto thee I shall do greater things that thou hast seen -- And hast thine eyes not seen that which I HAVE DONE? -- Hast thou not seen that which I have done? -- I say unto thee EACH ONE hast born witness of the things which I have done -- For thou hast walked with Me and I have counseled thee in ages past -- I have sat upon the mountain top with thee - and given unto thee the prophecies of these times - that Mine Word be fulfilled -- Thou art now upon this hallowed ground - for I have made it so -- I have made it hallowed by the WORD - and I have given unto thee Mine Word - that I should bring thee hence in that day when the time would be befitting - that Mine Work might go forth unto all the LANDS OF THE EARTH --

And it is NOW COME when I shall fulfill all the Word - for this is the day of fulfillment -- It shall be done as I have spoken - for it is the LAW -- It is given unto Me to know the LAW - and at no time shall I be off guard or found wanting -- I say unto thee - thine feet hast walked with Me over the same ground as thou now walk - and call thine place of abode -- Once thou didst dwell upon the site upon which now stands the place which I have established - wherein thou dost dwell -- So be it I shall fulfill Mine Covenant with thee ---

Let it be - for I shall give unto thee of Mine Cup that ye might drink and be satisfied --

So let it BE --

I AM the Lord thy God

Sananda

Recorded by Sister Thedra of The Emerald Cross

The Living Soul

Beloved Ones -- There is but One Father - GOD - The Cause of Our Being - and beside HIM there is no other Cause - for HE HAST BREATHED FORTH - and in that BREATH HE hast CAUSED thee to become a LIVING SOUL - and that is the part which is not seen by man - that which is not of flesh -- Yet onward and onward I shall lead thee into ever more glorious realms - greater that the "SOUL" - for the Soul too shall have ITS day - as well as its function - and then <u>it</u> shall be required of thee -- and greater realms shall ye explore - free from all form. As the Light shall ye be therein -- Ye shall be ONE with thine "SOURCE" - free from all form - yet taking that form which thou shall work with -- For it is said that ye shall do GREATER THINGS - it is so! For thou hast not imaged the magnitude of thine work - and ye shall be as I - neither bound nor born of flesh-- Never! Never again shall ye be born of the womb of woman - for I say unto thee it is finished! ---

I say unto thee - now pick up Mine Sandals - take up Mine Mantle and follow where I lead thee - for I have great things to show thee -- Be ye as ones prepared - for this do I now say COME!!

I shall lead thee gently but surely --

I AM Sananda

Recorded by Sister Thedra of The Emerald Cross

From Whence Cometh Our Help

Beloved Ones -- This day I would give unto thee - the part which I have kept for thee -- Yet the fullness of it thou could not bear - for thou art not <u>as</u> <u>yet</u> strong within the weaker parts -- The weaker parts shall be made strong - and thy weakness shall become thine strength -- So be it that I give unto thee as thou hast need - and at no time art thou alone -- At no time am I to be found asleep -- I say I am not a traitor - I remember that which I have said unto thee! Hast thou remembered Mine Words? - and hast thou given of thineself that ye might be as one prepared to receive me and of Me? ---

I say unto thee - reject not Mine hand which I proffer thee - for it is for thine own sake that I ask of thee - "Come" - that I stand with outstretched hand that I might give unto thee assistance - that I might lead thee out of bondage -- So be it that I am not alone -- There is a Mighty Host which stands ready to assist thee in thine ascent -- So let it be that they too might administer unto thee - it shall profit thee --

So be it that the Great and Mighty Council now sits in Council for the good of all which would partake of Their Love and Grace - of Their assistance -- Let it profit thee to accept Their assistance - for it is said They <u>Know</u> that which is wise and prudent for thee - They give not unto the unjust - for it would be the height of folly - for the foolish would but torment themself - <u>and</u> their fellow man -- So be it that <u>greater</u> things are in store for the just and prudent - which have reached the age of accountability ---

So be it I the Lord thy God hast spoken unto them which hast a mind to comprehend that which Spirit sayeth - for Spirit speaketh unto Spirit -- So let it Be for the GOOD OF ALL --

I AM Sananda

Recorded by Sister Thedra of The Emerald Cross

Mans Ingratitude & Mans Inheritance

Mine Children - O Mine Beloved Children -- This day I would have thee know that which I have Willed unto thee -- The fullness of Mine House is thine - and at no time have I denied thee - for I am a bountiful provider -- And at no time shall I be found wanting - yet it is given unto Mine Children to forget that I have sent them forth into the lands of the nations - and I have given unto them the lands and the seas -- And they have not given unto Me credit for that which I have spread before them as a bountiful gift --

While they have misused these gifts for vain glory and they have taken without that which I have provided them -- They have made of Mine Children/ (their brothers) slaves and paupers -- They betray themself in the doing - and give unto themself the bitter cup -- While I say unto thee - prepare for thineself the greater part - that which I have kept for thee - for I have kept the greater part for thine coming of age -- Now swiftly approaches thine age of accountability - when ye shall be brot in - and I shall place about thine shoulders the Royal Raiment - and I shall place upon thine head the Crown which shall signify thine Sonship ---

Ye shall stand upon Mine right hand - and I shall give unto thee thine inheritance in full -- Such is Mine Word unto thee this day -- So be it I have sent Mine Son unto thee and thou hast accepted Him in Mine Name -- NOW ye shall be as ones rewarded openly --

Solen Aum Solen

Recorded by Sister Thedra of The Emerald Cross

I am the Guardian of Thine Estate

Behold the LIGHT - SEE the things which I shall do -- And I have said unto thee - give unto Me that which is Mine - and I shall give unto thee that which is thine -- For I have kept for thee a goodly fortune - and no man shall pilfer it - or take it from Me - for I am the Guardian of thine fortune ---

While it is not yet known unto thee - the <u>fullness</u> thereof - I say it is a fortune far greater than that of the Kings of all the Earth combined lo it is so -- So be it I know whereof I speak - for the Kingdoms of men fall into decay - and pass - leaving but the fragments of remembrance - while I say unto thee - thine fortune shall not diminish neither shall it pass away -- For thou art inheritors of the Kingdom of God -- Let it BE For this hast it been given unto Me - to come unto thee that ye might be prepared to receive it -- So be it I Am the Son - sent of Mine Father that ye be prepared to return unto HIM with ME -So let it BE as HE hast WILLED IT.

I AM HE Which is known within the Inner Temple as Sananda

Recorded by Sister Thedra of The Emerald Cross

Bear Ye Witness of Me

Sori Sori - Hail! Hail - O ye Sons of God -- Let thine passport be <u>thine</u> passport - pass it not unto another - for I say unto thee - none else shall pass thereupon - for none enter unaware -- I say unto thee - thine passport shall not give unto another his entrance for it is given unto each to earn his passport - <u>each</u> <u>his</u> <u>own</u> -- And no man shall ride the back of another - for each shall carry his own self - his strength shall be his own - for none other shall he have --

For the time cometh when man shall learn the wisdom of self-preparation - and he shall give of himself that he be prepared - for none other prepareth him -- He shall know that his strength is given unto him as a gift - and he shall not misuse it - and he shall direct his energy into the right place -- Wherein he has his thots - therein he dwells -- I say unto thee - keep thine mind staid on ME - for I AM the Lord thy God - and I AM thine strength -- Thine strength cometh not of man - neither the food nor drink - for I am sufficient unto thee -- Bear ye witness of ME - and I shall give unto thee that which I have kept for thee ---

I AM Sananda

Recorded by Sister Thedra of The Emerald Cross

Freedom

Beloved Ones -- Mine hand is upon thee - and at no time shall I withdraw it from thee - for thou hast covenanted with Me - and I with thee -- Thou hast not remembered Our Covenant as I - yet I say ye shall come to remember - for I shall touch thee and ye shall be quickened - and ye shall remember ALL THINGS -- Time shall be no more - for ye shall be free from time --- And space shall be as naught - for ye shall transcend space -- Ye shall arise as on wings of LIGHT - and the gravitation of the Earth shall be as naught unto thee - for ye shall overcome the Law of Earth/ flesh/ matter/ time - and ye shall transcend ALL LAW - for ye shall BE -- Ye shall BE as thine Father hast

WILLED - ye shall have no fetters - no bondage -- For I say ye shall break all thine legirons - and come forth as Ones free from ALL BONDAGE -- So be it thine inheritance -- Let it be - for this have I come -- And I say unto thee - I am glad this day is come - when I might speak unto thee thusly ---

So be it I AM Sananda

The Lord thy God

Recorded by Sister Thedra of The Emerald Cross

Faith / Hope / Doubt / Knowing

Beloved of Mine Being -- This day I speak unto thee of "KNOWING"- and at no time shall I speak unto thee of faith - hope or doubt - for I speak unto thee that ye might have knowledge - that which is of the LIGHT - the Eternal Verities -- I say unto thee - it is for the good of ALL that I speak unto thee -- While it is given unto thee to be the One which is called as Mine Scribe - I say it is for the GOOD OF ALL that I speak -- Now let us consider faith as something hoped for - yet not received - while the Knower HAST RECEIVED ALREADY -- He hast accepted his gifts as the gifts of The Father - which hast sent him forth.

Now for that matter - after his receival he no longer hopes to receive he knows that he hast received - for he hast accepted -- His acceptance is not by word of mouth - but by every breath he draws - every breath he exhales -- He IS that which hast BECOME -- He becomes that which he hast hoped to BE - for this is the receiver of the gifts - and the one which hast accepted -- And he then becomes the KNOWER as well as the DOER - for he then steps forth with his Credentials - which no man sees with mortal eye -- No man can take from him his credentials - they can neither be pilfered or burned -- They can not be carried away by water or wind - neither buried within the Earth -- For that matter - they cannot be hidden from any man - for they are written upon his very Being -- He goes forth as ONE WHICH KNOWS - and he is not doubtful - fearful or swept by the foul winds which blow ---

He walketh with surety - knowing wherein he is staid - wherein he is kept -- I say he has at all times a willing mind -- He holds himself in readiness to serve his brothers - and he denies him <u>not</u> -- I say he knows wherein he is staid! So be it I shall <u>speak</u> again - for I come that there be UNDERSTANDING ---

Be it SO

I AM Sanat Kumara

Recorded by Sister Thedra of The Emerald Cross

I am the Captain of This Ship

Beloved -- It is Mine part to give unto thee this Word - and it shall profit them to receive it -- Let them which have ears to hear - hear that which I say to thee - for it is said for the good of all -- So be it that I am the Host of Hosts - the Lord of Lords - come that there be LIGHT - so let it BE -- Hold ye the Lamp which I give unto thee - high - hold it firm - steady - that it flicker not - that it be not fanned by the breeze -- I say hold ye steady the "LAMP" which I give unto thee - and let it not flicker by the breezes which blow - for many there be which blow -- And many a foul wind bloweth to and fro -- I say the stench of these foul winds shall not touch thee - for I am thine Shield and thine Buckler - and I shall show thee great and wonderful things --

For this have I said: "See ye the hand of God move - see the Work which I shall do"-- I am at the helm of this ship - and I am the Captain tried and true - fear not - for I know the turbulent seas whereupon the waters are troubled - and at no time shall I give unto thee the bitter cup -- I say unto thee - fear not - for I am with thee unto the end-- Let them which spit upon thee be - let them drink not of thine cup - for they have prepared for themself the cup which they would give unto thee -- Drink not of their bitter cup - partake not of it! - for therein is folly -- I say behold - the things which I shall do! - for I shall give unto thee that which they know not of - be it so --

And so be it I AM the Lord thy God

Sananda

Recorded by Sister Thedra of The Emerald Cross

Mine Cup Holds No Bitterness

Upon Mine High Holy Mountain I stand - and I see as from afar the groanings and the utterance of the <u>poor</u> <u>in</u> <u>spirit</u> -- They speak of and about Me - while they are wont to limit Me in Mine power -- They are prone to put words into Mine Mouth - and tie Mine hands - yet I say unto thee - Mine mouth shall spew their words out - and I shall give unto them no power -- For I am the Lord of Lords - and I am not to be given the bitter cup - I drink not of their mixtures - which they prepare for the ones which they would hold bound -- It is given unto Me to see them give unto their fellow men the bitter cup - and at no time shall I give unto Mine fellows the bitter cup -- Let thine lips touch Mine Cup and then ye shall know the sweetness thereof -- I say unto thee - Mine Cup holds for thee NO bitterness - drink ye thereof and I shall give unto thee greater capacity - that ye might drink deeply ---

So be it I AM

The Lord thy God

Sananda

Recorded by Sister Thedra of The Emerald Cross

The Rock

Beloved Ones -- This day I would say unto thee -- Bring thineself unto this Altar in holy benediction - that ye might receive the anointing - for it is said that I shall anoint thee - it is so -- So let it be-- Be ye not anxious - for I shall keep Mine Word unto thee -- Hold ye fast - and fear not - for I am thine Shield and thine Buckler -- I am the "Rock" upon which <u>This</u> <u>Temple</u> is builded - and I shall not be moved by the foul winds which bloweth across the lands-- I shall stand - when all else shall fail -- So be it I AM the Lord thy God ---

So be it I AM

Sananda

Recorded by Sister Thedra of The Emerald Cross

Duality
Male - Female

Beloved of Mine Being -- In the beginning there was ONE - The Father Of Himself He created <u>two</u> -- The two wast both male and female - and therein is a mystery unto man - for man hast not known this part of "The Plan" - for man hast not known himself as the ONE - he hast seen himself as <u>part</u> of the ONE -- Yet he shall come to know that he is not a thing apart - that he is a whole creature - and not divided against himself ---

Now when he went forth into darkness - when he went forth into bondage - he divided himself in twain - and at no time have I said this is <u>not</u> <u>so</u> - for it <u>is</u> SO -- Man hast divided himself in twain - and he shall at last be made whole - for he wast thus created - wast made perfect -- Neither male - neither female wast he --

Then there came a moment when he took upon himself the mind of man - he wast bi-sexual - yet without <u>desire</u> or passion - for he had nothing which tormented him - he wast <u>one</u> with himself - and he knew himself to BE WHOLE - NOT AS TWO but contained within himself the WHOLE -He had no passions which tormented him - no Longings which beset him -- Now I say unto thee - man hast long been tormented by his separation - he hast willed it so -- So be it he shall return unto his rightful estate - and he shall no more wander from planet to planet in his return - for he shall be brot out and given his inheritance - and he shall rejoice that his wandering is ended -- His longing shall no more torment him - for he shall be satisfied -- So be it I say unto thee - ye shall come to know the fullness of Mine Word unto thee this day ---

So be it I shall speak again of this subject --

I AM Sananda

Recorded by Sister Thedra of The Emerald Cross

Thine Return

Mine Beloved Children -- I say unto thee - the day cometh when ye shall again come to know Me as thou once did - for thou hast gone from Me as ones which knew Me -- And for this hast thine longing been great - thou hast been as ones away -- Yet I have not been unmindful of thee - in thine days of wandering and longing - for I say unto thee I have held thee fast -- As thine Mother - I have nourished thee and held thee unto Mine Eternal Bosom -- Now ye shall be as ones blest to return unto thine rightful estate - wherein there is no longing - for I say unto thee - thine longing shall be no more ---

So be it I shall receive thee as Mine own - and I shall be glad for thine return -- I say there are many which await thine return - these remember thee before thine going out into darkness -- I say unto thee - keep thineself in readiness - for it cometh to pass - that which I have proclaimed unto thee ---

So be it I AM thine

Eternal Mother

Recorded by Sister Thedra of The Emerald Cross

Each has a Place - Number - Color

Beloved Ones -- Mine Word unto thee this day would be: "Pour out the wine of great strength - that I might fill thine vessels unto overflowing with the '"Water of Life'" ---

I say unto thee - I have the Water which quenches thine thirst - and ye shall thirst no more -- So be it that I have kept the GREATER part for thee - I have kept the part which I have for thee - and I say unto thee thine part shall be as none other - for each is different - like unto none other -- For that matter - none shall be liken unto no other - for each hast been given a part which is THEIRS - and it is not be coming unto any other ---

For each hast a part - a color - a number - and a place - yet each fits into the plan as a whole - in perfect harmony - perfect peace - perfect union -- Perfect shall it be - for none shall be brot into the place of Mine Abode which does not fit into the plan ---

It is said: "Be ye prepared" - so be it ye shall be prepared - and ye shall will it so -- When thou hast so prepared thineself - I shall touch thee and ye shall see - and know thine part -- It is said: "Be ye at peace and wait upon ME the Lord thy God and I shall do that which I have said I shall do - for I am not a liar - neither am I a traitor - I betray not Mineself or Mine trust "-- Forget not that which I have said unto thee - for I am come that ye be prepared - so let it BE ---

I AM Sananda

Recorded by Sister Thedra of The Emerald Cross

There is but One Lord God

Beloved Ones -- This is Mine day - the day of The Lord - and it is for this that I say unto thee - prepare thineself -- There is but ONE LORD GOD - and I AM HE -- Know ye that there are many which claim that they are He - yet these are but the false ones which would but mislead thee -- I say unto thee - thou art fortuned to be Mine hand-maidens - and I have said that ye shall do that which I have given unto thee to do and it shall profit thee - it shall be for thine own sake that I stand by -- While Mine inheritance hast been given unto Me in full - I say thou hast not as yet been given in full - thou hast not as yet accepted THINE inheritance - and thou art as yet bound -- While I am free and I know thine own capacity - thine limitations - I have said all thine limitations shall be removed - for I shall touch thee and they shall go!---

While I ask of thee nothing except obedience unto the law - and ye shall be as ones willing to follow where I lead thee -- So be it I know wherein the pitfalls lie - so be it I am come that I might lead thee aright So be it I am prepared for that which is to come - I am prepared to deliver thee ---

I AM Sananda

Recorded by Sister Thedra of The Emerald Cross

The Director
Gives His Blessings

Blest be this day -- Blest be this hour -- Blest be the labour of thine hand -- Blest be the hands of the laborers - for they shall do that which is given unto them to do -- Blest be the Work which shall be given them for it shall bring forth the NEW DAY in all of its glory -- For these Mine Servants shall BE the laborers in Mine vineyards - and they too shall partake of the harvest - and it shall be a <u>Mighty</u> one - greater than any other the Earth hast <u>ever</u> <u>known</u> ---

So be it that I know - for I am the Lord thy God - and I am well qualified to speak unto thee of the NEW DAY - for I am the Director of the "NEW DISPENSATION" -- I have called thee forth and given unto thee certain parts - and certain parts have I given unto each of thee yet these parts are not at variance - they are part of the WHOLE PLAN and none shall rebel for their part - none shall covet the part which is given another -- For the greater part is not the part of the traitor or the wonton - For his rebellion does he betray himself or his trust -- When it is said: Give unto thineself NOT the "Bitter Cup" - see that which is said -- Comprehend that which is said - and know ye that which is said! and let not thine foot slip -- I say - let not thine foot slip - for the way is strait and narrow -- So be it and Selah ---

Hold ye steadfast - and I shall lead thee all the way ---

So be it I AM

The Lord thy God

Sananda

Recorded by Sister Thedra of The Emerald Cross

No Parting Have We Known

Beloved Of Mine Being -- This day is the day for which thou hast waited -- Thou hast waited long for THIS DAY-- This is the day of The Lord - in which I go forth as One prepared to gather up Mine people - "Mine flock" - MINE - "Mine own" - for they are of Mine origin - like unto ME -

And for this do I say: "Beloved of Mine Being" - for thou art of Me and We know no separation -- NO parting have We known - no time have We known - and no distance have We known - We are ONE -- Therefore thine suffering is Our suffering - thine longing Our longing thine sorrow is Ours ---

Behold the LIGHT and be ye ONE OF US - and know ye that ye stand not along - NEVER ALONE! ---

For We stand ready to assist thee in thine return unto thine rightful estate -- Behold! I say Behold! the GLORY OF THE LORD - and know ye that there is a plan - and within that plan thou dost have thine BEING So be it that I am One of "THE SEVEN LIGHTS"- I am One of THE SEVEN - Which hast held thee within the palm of Mine hand - and I shall stand ready to bring thee out of bondage - when thine sojourn is ended-- Thou has gone out of thine own _free_ _will_ - and thou hast willed that ye be brot back! Yet there is a law which decides that which ye call TIME -- Yet time is of thine realm -- Our realm knows no time - for Us there is no law governing - or _making_ time - for time AS thou knowest it - is non-existent -- Yet there are cycles which far surpasses thine time it is the "time" of going out and coming in -- These are the cycles of which We speak - and thou art under the illusion of thine time - of day and night - of the seasons- yet the seasons We speak of - are the ones of bringing in and sending out - the going forth and the returning---

Let the going forth be as the returning - a time of joy and great LIGHT and strength -- Love the seasons - for each brings a time of fulfillment - a time of great joy and illumination ---

Be ye as ones prepared for thine return - for many await thee ---

So be it I AM thine Elder Brother

Sanat Kumara

Recorded by Sister Thedra of The Emerald Cross

I Shall Open Up Mine Store

Beloved Ones -- While it is thine part to give unto others - these Mine Words - it is theirs to receive it -- It is Mine part to give unto thee - and in like manner does the Word become manifest -- As the Word goes out before Me - it is made manifest - and that which I have set forth becomes apparent unto thee ---

It is said that as ye receive - so shall ye give unto others -- So be it as ye have received - so shall ye give - and for this shall thine capacity be increased - I say unto thee thine CAPACITY shall be increased -- So be it I shall give unto thee in full measure - pressed down and running over -- So be it that they shall come that they might partake of thine portion - and it shall be portioned out unto them - and they shall be glad for their "Portion" - for it shall profit them -- Hear ye that which

I say unto thee - and be ye as ones prepared to receive thine portion with increase! -- So be it that I shall open up Mine wares - and I shall show unto thee Mine Store - and I shall withhold nought - for Mine Gems I shall give unto thee - and Mine Pearls I shall bestow upon thee and I shall withhold nought from thee -- And it shall be as the treasure house of thine own - wherein thou shall find many things which have been put therein for thine coming of age -- Let it be a great and glad age - for I say - the time approaches when ye shall be as ones responsible for thineself - and I shall give unto thee thine inheritance in full -- So be it I have awaited this day ---

Let it be for this day that I speak --

I bless thee with Mine

Presence - I AM

Sananda

Recorded by Sister Thedra of The Emerald Cross

Praise / Blessings

Behold in ME the LIGHT Which I AM - and know ye wherein thou art staid - for in ME thou art staid -- I say unto thee - Behold the LIGHT Which I AM - and KNOW from whence cometh thine strength -- Hear ye that which I say unto thee - and be ye as ones blest -- For have I not placed upon thee Mine Seal? Have I not paid unto thee homage? Have I not given unto thee Mine benediction? Have I not given unto thee of Mine Cup? Have I not given unto thee of Mineself that ye be blest? --

So be it that I am come that ye be lifted up - that ye be prepared to go where I go -- So let Us rejoice together ---

I say: Come let Us rejoice together -- Praise ye the Name of Solen Aum Solen --

Praise ye the Name of Solen Aum Solen -

Praise HIM ALL who hear Mine Words -

Let thine Praise fill the Earth --

Recorded by Sister Thedra of The Emerald Cross

Come Home - Tarry No More

Beloved - O - Beloved Children -- Art thou not the fulfilling of Mine own longing - Art thou not the fulfilling of Mine own Heart - Hast thou not been given the Kingdom of "Thine Father" - Am I not the "Father" first and last?

Hast thou remembered that which I have said unto thee in the time of thine going out?

I didst say unto thee - "Know thineself - forget not thine inheritance and return unto Me as thou hast gone out" -- Yet thou hast tarried upon the brink - and thou hast dragged thine feet - WEARY of the flesh-- Yet I say unto thee - "Come - Come Home! -- Come home - tarry no more -- Hasten ye to return unto ME - and no more shall ye go into bondage -- Never again shall ye take upon thineself the garment of dense substance - thru the womb of woman -- For thou shall be free -

even as Mine Son Sananda - Which I have sent forth that ye might know that thou art not alone!

So be it MANY A SON have I sent that ye might know - yet thou hast tarried in flesh - body after body -- Many bodies/ vehicles of flesh hast thou taken unto thineself -- As the cloak of disguise hast thou worn these shoddy garments of flesh - forgetting that thou art not flesh - that thou art of the PURE ESSENCE of MINESELF ---

Thou art of "The First Born" - and at no time have I denied thee ---

Thou hast wearied of thine cloak of flesh - it hast tormented thee - weighed heavily upon thee - yet thou hast not awakened unto the fullness of thine inheritance - that which I have WILLED unto thee in the beginning ---

NOW I say unto thee - make ye haste - linger no longer - for this hast Mine Son Sananda revealed Himself unto thee -- Be ye up and alert thineself and come forth THIS DAY - as ones prepared to return unto ME with Him ---

NOW let it be said that I weary not of flesh - I despise NOT flesh - yet I say unto thee - I have the greater part for thee - and thou shall walk the greater heights - free from the denser flesh - the atomic structure of flesh -- For I say ye shall wear the garments of LIGHT SUBSTANCE and these shall not bind thee -- I prepare a place upon Mine right hand and I bid thee enter in and partake of Mine fare - and I say unto thee FARE THEE WELL! for I have prepared a bountiful fortune for thee - and ye shall not want -- Partake of Mine Substance - and be ye as ones prepared to receive thine inheritance in full ---

Know ye that I hold them within MINE BOSOM - and I shall not sacrifice thee - for I AM thine

Eternal Parent

Solen Aum Solen

Recorded by Sister Thedra of The Emerald Cross

Be Ye as The Light

Behold Mine Children! Behold ye Mine Children - cradled in ME - CRADLED IN ME! - for I AM HE Which hast brot thee forth -- I AM HE Which holds thee fast -- And I say unto thee - I AM thine Parent Eternal --- Hold ye the LIGHT which I have endowed unto thee - hold it high - and be ye as ones which know wherein thou art staid --

Let thine LIGHT shine - and be ye as the LIGHT which shines forth - that all might see and know that thou art of the "First Born" -- For the LIGHT shall not be hidden - and nothing shall dim it from the eyes of the ones which have been CAUSED to see - So be it ye shall know each other - and ye shall partake of the same Goblet -- For I say unto thee - the Goblet shall be presented unto thee - and it shall be filled to overflowing - and ye shall drink and be satisfied -- So be it ye shall thirst no more - for all thine thirst shall be satisfied ---

Now I place before thee a table - spread with the good things of Mine House - and ye shall be partakers thereof - and at no time shall ye be denied -- So be it that I bid thee partake of Mine Board - and ye shall not want ---

Be ye blest forevermore --

I AM thine

Parent Eternal

Recorded by Sister Thedra of The Emerald Cross

O Mine Sons - Come Home

Hail! Hail! unto thee - O Sons of Israel! Hail O Mighty SONS! Be ye blest this day -- Let this day be the day of thine return -- COME! Let it be <u>this day</u> -- And hear ye the GLAD TIDINGS - THE SON IS RETURNED -- Let thine wanderings be ended --

O- Mine SONS thou art NOT alone - for many await thine coming let it BE THIS DAY ---

When thine wandering shall end - IT SHALL END IN THINE VICTORY!

This hast been said many times - yet thou knowest not the joy of thine return - for it is yet fortuned unto thee to be under the law of flesh and flesh cannot comprehend the freedom of SPIRIT - MINE SPIRIT!

Hear ye - Mighty Sons! Hear ye - for I have spoken the WORD - COME HOME! - Come HOME unto thine final "WORK" - the WORK which shall be thine inheritance - wherein ye shall be free to go and come unto any place - any realm - <u>without</u> the bounds of that realm -- Wherein hast thou found freedom in flesh? I say unto thee - freedom does not belong unto flesh - it is of Spirit -- Let it be according to the

LAW that thou art unbound - for this hast I given unto thee - the law - transgress it not ---

Be ye blest of Mine Sons - and be ye as ones prepared to receive of Mine Sons - for They STAND BY to assist thee - This is MINE WORD and I have spoken it - and it hast been received and recorded this day - upon which I have placed Mine Seal ---

I AM thine

Parent Eternal

Recorded by Sister Thedra of The Emerald Cross

Judge Not

Beloved Ones -- The Word I would give unto thee this day - would be for the good of all mankind - and it would be the Word which should profit thee ---

When it is given unto One to take up the garments of flesh - it is for the purpose of creating the essence of experience within that realm -- The essence of experience - is the accumulated experience by which one judges righteous judgement - for without the experience one knows not -- For without he KNOWS - he cannot judge righteous judgement Therefore I say unto them which KNOW NOT - "Judge NOT" - for thou knowest NOT!

Now when it is come that ye know - there will be understanding - and then ye shall be as ones prepared to go forth amongst thine fellowmen and administer unto them - for without understanding thine ministry is as nought - for it is not given unto thee to be as ones prepared for preparedness is understanding - of the nature of man - the law - the word - thine own self - and therein is A KEY -- I say unto them which I have called - here is the KEY -- and I bid thee pass within the door which I AM - and therein ye shall be as one with ALL - ALL with ONE Which I AM - then ALL things shall be made known unto thee ---

Be ye as ONE - be ye ONE with ME and fear not - for I AM HE Which is sent - and I and Mine Father is/ are ONE - for from HIM I have received MINE Credentials - I have received Mine passport into HIS place of abode --- I have received of HIM Mine Inheritance ---

So be it I AM the Lord of Lords the Host of Hosts

Sananda

Recorded by Sister Thedra of The Emerald Cross

Thy Will Be Done

Beloved Ones -- Upon this day I say unto thee - I have established this Mine Temple - and I shall fill it unto overflowing -- For I shall bring forth many which shall sing praise unto the Lord of Hosts - for I shall put into thine mouth the words which shall fill their hearts with great joy - and they shall be the fruits of thine labor ---

I say unto thee - I have sent thee forth as ones prepared - and as thou hast received - so shall ye give -- So be it that I am prepared to give unto thee in great measure -- So let it be for the good of ALL ---

I AM come that there be LIGHT - so let it BE

I AM Sananda

Recorded by Sister Thedra of The Emerald Cross

The Counterpart

Beloved - O - Mine Beloved One -- While it is given unto Me to be the Lord of Lords - the Host of Hosts - it is given unto thee to be One of the Host - one which hast taken upon self - flesh - flesh of Earth - Earth Substance - Substance of Earth - dense and heavy -- While I am the Counterpart-- LIGHT am I - and flesh is not Mine - for I am of the Spirit -- While Spirit hinders not - flesh binds -- While it weighs heavy Spirit is LIGHT and ever present - neither does it go or come - It IS - and IT is not limited - neither am I - for that matter ---

I speak unto thee as the Lord of Lords - as The Lord God - and I bid thee come forth - that ye too might stand with Me upon Mine High Holy Mountain - wherein ye might see the plan - even as I see -- I say greater heights shall ye gain - for this have I said COME -- So let it BE as The Father hast willed it ---

I AM that I AM

Sananda

Recorded by Sister Thedra of The Emerald Cross

Bondage & Freedom

Mine Children - Children of THE LIGHT! -- I say unto thee: "THOU ART CHILDREN OF THE LIGHT!" -- I say unto thee THIS DAY - thou art bound by Mine LOVE Which knows no circumference! ---

I tell thee of a surety - thou art held fast by Mine Love which is boundless! ---

Hear ye O Mine Children!! - For I have sent thee forth as ones perfect -- Now I say ye shall return unto ME - unscathed - unharmed - as thou shall be NO LESS for having gone into bondage -- For I have willed unto thee a goodly fortune - and it is not spent - it hast not dissipated itself - for it is intact - <u>yea</u> and <u>with</u> <u>interest</u> -- I bid thee arise claim thine Sonship and return unto ME even as thou hast gone out from ME -- And great shall be the joy which shall ring out as a mighty sound - So let it RING! -- Let it ring - for the Earth and the Heavens shall declare the joy -- So be it I have spoken and thou hast heard ME.

I AM thine Eternal Parent

Solen Aum Solen

Recorded by Sister Thedra of The Emerald Cross

The Victory

Beloved Ones -- This day let it be understood that thou art the "SONS OF GOD" -- Fortuned unto thee is the greatest of ALL fortunes - for it is said: Thou shall return unto ME - unharmed - unscathed - and pure even as thou hast gone out from ME -- I tell thee it is given unto Me to know thine fortune - thine wanderings - thine longings - and for this have I said unto thee - <u>it shall end</u> - so let it end in thine Victory -- Be ye mindful of that which I have said unto thee - and be ye as ones prepared to return unto thine abiding place -- Arise! Come Home! - and be ye as one which hast overcome -- I say unto thee: Hail! Hail O- Ye Mighty Sons of Israel -- Be ye blest THIS DAY ---

So be it I AM The Lord thy God -

Sananda

Recorded by Sister Thedra of The Emerald Cross

I See It as Done

Holy - Holy is the Word - and great the power thereof-- Bless thineself with the Word - by the Word - for this is it given unto thee -- See the manifestation thereof - give of thineself that it be manifest - for I say unto thee - thou art THE WORD made flesh ---

I say - Thou ART THE WORD made flesh!

Behold ye the flesh made manifest -- I say unto thee - the Word shall be made manifest before THEE - SEE IT -- Know ye that I have spoken unto thee this day - of the power of THE WORD -- Now I say unto thee - stand ye steadfast - and watch and see - that which I have done -- I say unto thee - thou art Sons of God - gone forth as One in Spirit - as Spirit made flesh -- I say unto thee - AS SPIRIT MADE FLESH - for the SPIRIT hast taken upon Itself flesh - by and thru the

WORD - THE SPOKEN WORD -- It is said thou shall return unto thine abiding place and I say - I see it as done -- Be ye blest of Me and by Me this day ---

So be it I AM

Sananda

Recorded by Sister Thedra of The Emerald Cross

Enter into the Courts of The King of Kings

Beloved Ones -- This day let it be understood that there is but ONE LORD GOD - and that there is but ONE GOD THE FATHER of Us - of US ALL - which have emanated out from HIM -- We are HIS - of HIM - and no man changeth that which is of HIM - for by HIS POWER HIS LOVE - HIS GRACE hast HE sent forth that which HE hast called "SONS"-- Sons of God art We - We are by HIS GRACE <u>men</u> - MEN! and by His Grace are We His Sons!!---

Sons of God shall we ever be! -- Now I say unto thee - hear ye Me and be ye aware of THINE DIVINITY -- Arise from out the mire of the world of darkness - which is the creation of man - and claim thine SONSHIP - for I say unto thee - it is thine by Divine Inheritance - and it is not robbery to claim that which HE THE FATHER ETERNAL hast WILLED unto thee -- I say ye shall arise - and come forth as ones prepared to enter into the Courts of thine ROYAL KING -- The KING OF KINGS hast prepared for thee a place - and thine R<u>oy</u>al R<u>aiment</u> awaits thee -- Come! Come! and hasten ye! - put on the WHOLE ARMOR of God -- Girdle up thine loins and make ye haste - and be ye about thine Fathers business - for HE hast said Come! COME!! and thou hast tarried long - thou hast tarried LONG!! -- Now ye shall come forth as ones prepared - yet ye shall WILL IT SO! ---

Be ye as ones mindful of thine Divinity -- Walk ye with surety- and BLESS THINESELF in the doing---

Be ye blest of Me and by Me - for I am The One sent that ye might awaken! --

SO LET IT BE -

I AM Sananda

Recorded by Sister Thedra of The Emerald Cross

Understanding

Beloved Ones -- This day - I speak unto thee of understanding - and with understanding -- It is for Mine understanding that I am able to say unto thee that which is profitable unto thee ---

Now let it be said: that understanding comes from knowing - and to know is to understand -- It is for this that I speak unto thee - that ye might have understanding/ that ye might KNOW ---

So be it I am the One sent that this BE - so let it BE ---

It is with understanding of that which IS - that I say unto thee - "Drink from Mine Chalice" - and with understanding of that which shall be accomplished when I say unto thee - go ye forth as Mine hand

153

and Mine foot made manifest unto <u>them</u> which ask of thee -- Let it be as Mine Word that they might be fed - even as thou art fed -- Now I say unto thee - thine hand shall be Mine hand - thine Word Mine Word - for I shall put Mine Word into thine mouth - and they shall be as ones prepared to receive Mine Word-- So be it that I have sent thee forth as ones prepared -- So be it that I fill thine Cup to overflowing - and I give unto thee sufficient that they might drink of the overflow - and they shall find it satisfying - so be it and Selah ---

I go before thee to prepare the Way before thee-- Tarry not -- Weary not ---

Be ye blest this day --

I AM WITH THEE -

Sananda

Recorded by Sister Thedra of The Emerald Cross

THE FIRST GENERATION

Beloved Ones -- Whither goest thou? From whence comest thou? -- Now I say unto thee - thou art the Ones sent forth as the Sons of God - a generation set apart - and sent forth as the Ones designated as "Sons of God" -- And let it be understood that not all have the Mark of the "Son" upon him - for I say unto thee - not all are of the First Born - THE FIRST GENERATION ---

Let it be understood that the First Generation went out perfect and complete - Whole - and these knew themself to BE WHOLE - ONE with their SOURCE --

Now it is come when there shall be a great awakening - for the sleep shall be no more - it shall pass - and ye shall remember thine ONENESS and thine perfect state of BEINGNESS - and thine dreams shall be as nought -- Let them pass and be no more - for I say they shall torment thee no more ---

Be ye not anxious - for I AM the Lord of Lords - the Host of Hosts and I shall direct thee in thine every move -- While it is said ye shall be as ones prepared - that I might come in and sup with thee - I shall give of Mine Cup - that ye might sup with ME --

So let US drink of the WATER OF LIFE and rejoice that this day is come ---

So be it that I am come --

Come - let Us rejoice together --

Sananda

Recorded by Sister Thedra of The Emerald Cross

For Thine Rememberance

Sori Sori -- While it is given unto thee to be Sons of The MOST HIGH LIVING GOD - I say unto thee - thou art as ones which have thine memory blanked from thee-- Yet it SHALL be restored unto thee - and nothing shall be hidden from thee - I say ALL things shall be remembered -- And for this shall I the Lord thy God touch thee - and ye shall receive of ME as I have received of Mine Father -- So be it ye shall know as I know - and ye shall no more go into darkness ---

Now I say unto thee - rest in the knowing that I am the ONE sent that ye be prepared for the greater part -- So be it I am HE which hast gone before thee that the way be made clear before thee -- So be it I shall show thee many things which hast not been revealed unto thee -- For this I say: "I shall open up Mine Storehouse wherein all things shall be shown thee".

Be ye at Peace

for I AM with thee -

Sananda

Recorded by Sister Thedra of The Emerald Cross

The Rites of the Order of Melchezedek

Beloved Ones -- This day I would say unto thee - There is but ONE FATHER ETERNAL - One Lord God - One which hast come into "flesh" - as the forerunner of thine return - One which hast given unto thee the Rites of the Melchezedek Order -- And I say unto thee - the way is CLEAR before thee - and ye have but to open the door and enter into the Holy of Holies - for it is written that thou hast received thine passport into the Sacred Place wherein I abide ---

I speak unto thee of the "Order of Melchezedek" - it is given unto Me to be One of this Order - and I know of a certainty that which I say --- It is for this that I have given unto thee THE RITES of this ORDER - for it is by these RITES that thou art of the mind - the power - the authority to give unto others as thou hast received of ME---

Yet it shall be well that ye first know as I know - then ye shall know in full - NOT in part -- It shall be well that "they" first apply the LAW unto "themself" - then they shall be invited into the banquet table - that they might partake of the feast -- Yet it is said: "MANY ARE CALLED AND FEW ARE CHOSEN" Why? - for they have not heard THE WORD - they have not heeded that which hast been said - they have not applied the LAW unto themself -- It is said that ye first apply the Law unto thine own self - then ye shall be justified in giving it unto others -- Be ye as ones which have applied it and found it good - let not thine own foot slip -

Call not for them - before thou hast called for thineself -- Let it be for the good of all that ye call for thine own self - for art thou not one with thine "Brother"? So be it for his good that ye purify thine own self that ye better serve him ---

Such is Mine Word unto thee this day -- I am come that ye be blest so be it ---

I AM Sananda

Recorded by Sister Thedra of The Emerald Cross

The Order of Melchezedek

Beloved of Mine Being -- Let it be recorded for the record - that the Order of Melchezedek is that which IS -- Before the world wast fashioned it WAS - and in no wise wast it fashioned in the way of man of Earth - for man hast not fashioned such a School - such an Order ---

The Order of Melchezedek is that which was from the beginning of man's going out - as fashioned by Our Father Which is the Designer and the Author of its LAWS ---

I say: The Order of Melchezedek is the Highest Order known upon the planet of Earth - and for that matter - few know it or of it - for it is for the Initiate which hast learned the Law - for the one which hast applied the Law unto himself - and obeyed ALL the Laws set forth as stated in the LAW of The Order of Melchezedek -- This is stated simply and wisely - for it is not by design that the law be complicated - man complicates - and We are not the complicators -- Of man's opinions - confusions We are no part --

It is by design that the LAW is simply stated - and at no time do We force the opinions of man upon thee - for they are as the legirons which We would but cut away that ye be free -For this have We given unto thee the Law - that ye might be free from all bondage ---

So be it that I shall speak at length on the Order of Melchezedek at a later time --

I am One sent that this BE - so let it be ---

Such is Mine Word unto thee this day ---

I AM Sananda

>Recorded by Sister Thedra of The Emerald Cross

Be Ye as Ones Returned

Beloved Children -- Children of Mine Own Bosom art thou - Thou hast wandered long and far - while thou hast dreamed strange dreams -- Thou hast wearied of thine wanderings- yet I have not wearied of Mine waiting -- I wait thine return unto thine rightful estate- THINE ESTATE which- IS THINE by Divine right - for thou art Children of the Most High Living God -- And not one of Mine Children shall be lost sight of - for I know where they sleepeth - and I know wherein they toil for bread - wherein they suffer and sorrow ---

While I say unto them COME HOME - COME HOME - they stir not - yet it is the day of awakening -- I say - no more shall Mine Children go into bondage -- For this have I sent forth a fiat - ARISE! COME! - COME HOME and be ye as ones returned unto thine rightful ESTATE - for I have given unto thee a princely fortune and ye shall accept it in Mine Name - and by Mine Grace shall it be -- Let thine hand be Mine -- Mine hand shall bring thee back even as it sent thee forth - be ye as ones returned!

I AM thine FATHER ETERNAL

Solen Aum Solen

Recorded by Sister Thedra of The Emerald Cross

Ye are of the Light - See It

Beloved Ones -- This day let it be known that I AM COME - that I AM not afar off - that I am the Lord God - that there is LIGHT -- I say ye are of THE LIGHT - SEE IT - and be ye as ones unbound - by that which hast held thee fast -- Let it be said that the dragon hast no <u>power</u> over thee -- So be it I am come that ye be delivered out of BONDAGE So let it suffice that I know thee to be Mine Own - one of Mine flock - I shall pluck them out one by one - yea three by three's I shall pluck them out - and I shall give unto them as I have received of Mine Father for HE hast given unto ME Mine inheritance <u>in</u> <u>full</u> --

So be it that I am the Keeper of thine inheritance - it is not spent! <u>It</u> is intact and awaits <u>thee</u> - thine coming - let it be as The Father hast willed it! for HE hast set thee aside and hast fortuned unto thee a great fortune - befitting the Sons of God -- And ye shall return unto Him fully accountable for thineself - and ye shall be clothed in Royal Raiment - and there shall be great joy and great and powerful music shall fill the Cosmos-- For it is said - that when a Son returns there is great joy thruout all the Cosmos.

I say <u>Come</u> let Us rejoice! Come let Us rejoice together - for it is now come when ye <u>shall</u> return unscathed - unharmed - as ones purified and justified ---

I say unto thee: "Pass ye in - and let Us rejoice for <u>this</u> <u>day</u> - it shall bring forth the glad tidings and the echo of: 'Hail! Hail - a Son hast returned!' - 'Hail unto the Victor! - for a Mighty Victory is won this day!"---

Be ye as ones prepared for I shall give unto thee the cup from which I have drunken - and from which I have sup't - let it suffice thee - for it shall be filled to overflowing!

Let it BE

I AM

Sananda

Recorded by Sister Thedra of The Emerald Cross

The Lamp

Beloved -- This I would say unto thee this day - it is for thine sake that I say unto thee ARISE - and be ye as ones blest - for it is NOW COME when ye shall place thine feet upon higher ground -- Ye shall arise and stand as on the ROCK - and ye shall know that which hast not been yet revealed unto thee -- I say ye shall stand with Me upon the Mountain Top - and ye shall see afar - and know that which ye see - and at no time shall ye be confused - ye shall comprehend that which ye shall see.

Now I say - Behold the Hand of God - see it move - and be ye blest. Hold firm the Lamp which I have placed within thine hands - for the Lamp which I give unto thee is filled to capacity - it shall not fail thee. Be ye blest this day ---

I AM Sananda

Recorded by Sister Thedra of The Emerald Cross

Sananda: To the Father

Holy - Holy - O Mine Father! Holy art Thou -- For this I am Thine - Wholy Thine - for Thou hast given unto ME BEING -- Thou art ME - and in THEE I Am staid ---

Blest am I - O Mine Father! Gracious art Thou -- Wilt these Thine Children not come to know THEE as I know Thee ---

I say unto them - they shall come to know Thee even as I know Thee - and it is so - so shall it be unto Thine Glory - for it is by Thine Grace that it shall be ---

So let it be as Thou hast Willed it ---

I am Thine Son - sent that it be so -- I have touched them that they be blest of ME as Thou hast blest ME - O Father ---

I ask nothing save obedience unto the Law ---

I ask of them nought that I have not done -- So be it that they return unto Thee with Me - The Host of Hosts --- I AM Sananda

So be it I AM The One sent that it BE

So shall it be unto Thine Glory O Father

Recorded By Sister Thedra

The Third Watch

Hail - Hail unto The King of Glory! He cometh at the Third Watch - I say - unto the Third Watch He cometh -- Hail - Hail unto The King of Glory!

Be ye as ones blest to receive HIM - for HE hast come -- It is now the Third Watch - I say LOOK! LISTEN! SEE! and KNOW!

For this have I said - be ye as ones prepared-- And unto them which art prepared I shall set Mine Seal upon them - and they shall pass into the Holy of Holies with Me - for I am The King of Glory and I am come.

I say unto thee this day - make it known unto all people that I AM COME!

I am come that the WAY be made strait before thee -- Come follow ye ME ---

I am The King of Kings -

The King of Glory -

So shall it ever BE -

I AM Sananda

Recorded by Sister Thedra of The Emerald Cross

The Order of Melchezedek

Beloved Ones -- This day let it be said that the Order of Melchezedek is the <u>oldest</u> and the Greatest Order known upon the Earth -- And it is given unto Me to know - for I am One of that Order -- I am come that ye might come to know as I <u>know</u> - for this have I given unto thee the Law - the keeping of Mine sayings - and the guardianship of Mine sobrieties -- I say - I am come that ye might COME TO KNOW as I know ---

For it is given unto Me to KNOW the fullness of "The Plan" -- I tell thee of a surety - there is no mystery With Me - for I am aware of all 'the plan' - and I am in no wise a silent member of <u>this</u> <u>Order</u> - for I speak out - and I Am speaking out that man might come to know his <u>true</u> identity and his full Sonship -- At no time have I withheld Mine love from him - yet he hast not prepared himself for the Greater Part -- It is said that I shall reveal Mineself unto them which are prepared to receive ME AND OF ME - so be it that I know them - I am not deceived! ---

Neither do I enter into the dens of iniquity - I call them out! I say: "Come!" and they shall come forth - and THEN I shall give unto them as they are prepared to receive -- So be it that I am the One sent that they be brot forth - out of darkness/ bondage---

So be it that I shall speak again and again of this Order -- Be ye as one prepared - for I shall give unto thee in great measure ---

I AM Sananda

Recorded by Sister Thedra of The Emerald Cross

Authority to Set Up the School of Melchezedek

Beloved Ones -- This day I say unto thee - Behold the Power of "The Word" - for it shall bring forth Great manifestations such as man hast not seen ---

I say: This is "The New Day" in which great progress shall be made for man hast been asleep - in lethargy - as ones dead upon his feet -- Now it is come when they shall alert themself - and come forth as ones prepared for a greater work.

And the "Work" shall be as the Work of The Father - for it shall profit all men - it shall be for the GOOD of all -- And there shall be Great and Grand things accomplished in the time just ahead -- For I have sent forth Mine Emissaries - and I have given unto them the power and Authority to set up The School of Melchezedek -- Within their realm it shall be made known that there is such a School --

And there shall be a great number from amongst the world of men inquiring of such a School - and ye shall give unto them that which I have given unto thee for them -- For I say unto thee - thou hast been obedient unto the LAW - and obeyed every commandment - and thou hast proven thineself trustworthy - and at no time hast thou denied Me

- neither Mine Words -- Mine sayings have been HARD - yet they are thine rod and thine staff ---

I say unto thee - there shall be many inquiring of Me and the School of Melchezedek - and they too shall learn obedience - and how they might be freed of all bondage -- So be it that I have spoken unto these present - these which are within the sound of THESE MINE WORDS.

So let them which read - take heed and be as ones which have comprehension of these Words - for without comprehension there is no understanding - and to understand is to know ---

While it is given unto Me to be the Director of this New Dispensation - I am free to speak unto thee of The School of Melchezedek - for I am the Head of this School - and I prepare Mine "Sibors" - Mine people - Mine Disciples - that they be prepared for such Work as I do -- I am not so foolish as to give Mine Pearls unto babes - which know not their worth -- I ask of thee nought save obedience unto the Law set forth - within the portions allotted thee -- It is given unto Me to know each and every One by Name - by number - by color - and I am not deceived -- It is not given unto Me to sleep - for I sleep not - I know - for this I speak unto thee thusly ---

Arise! and be ye as ones prepared to go where I lead thee ----

I have said unto thee: The door stands ajar - pass ye in and partake of Mine Board - for I am a generous Host -- Be ye as ones welcome - for I have placed Mine Seal upon thee - and by that Seal shall ye be known ---

I AM the Host of Hosts -

I AM The Lord thy God

Sananda

Recorded by Sister Thedra of The Emerald Cross

A Son is Returned

Beloved Ones -- See ye the hand of God move - know ye that it moveth- and give ye heed unto the working thereof -- For THIS DAY - I say unto thee - there shall be a great awakening amongst all the nations of the Earth -- And it shall be as the LIGHT floods the Earth - for the Light shall fill the 'LANDS' - and the great onrush of LIGHT shall go forth unobstructed and uncovered -- And they which have not prepared themself for "This Day" shall be as ones removed into yet a remote place - wherein they shall be prepared ---

Yet there are ones which shall put aside the old garments of flesh - and they shall put on the new - and be as ones renewed - "Made Whole" And they shall walk as ones made new/ "Made Whole" - and they shall no more go into bondage - be born of woman -- And they shall be as ones prepared to enter into The Most Holy of Holies - wherein they might receive their inheritance in full -- So be it that there are ones now prepared for that - yet they are not fortuned the end of their "Mission" their time is not ended - for this they wait --

It is said their waiting shall be profitable unto them - for they shall be justified by and thru their waiting -- So be it I know their longing - and their going and coming - I see the grandeur of the end - So be it these shall be brot out in in the end - and they shall be put into a place wherein there are there are <u>many</u> which await their coming -- And great shall be the joy of all which have arisen - for they shall see and know that they have won the "<u>fight</u>" - the Victory hast been won - and the glad tidings shall go out - Hail! Hail! A Son is RETURNED! ---

So be it a Glad Anthem -

I Am Come that This Day may bear fruit --

So be it I AM

Sananda

     Recorded by Sister Thedra of The Emerald Cross

School of Melchezedek - Teachings

Beloved Ones -- While it is given unto thee to be as ones walking in flesh - I say unto thee - flesh hast not the power to bind thee - for the flesh is but the vehicle of Spirit - and Spirit is not contained within flesh Flesh is animated by - and of Spirit -- Let Us speak of Spirit - Wherein is it said that Spirit is <u>free</u> - and is not bound by anything - it knows no bounds ---

For this do I speak unto thee of freedom - and of Spirit - for the Spirit sayeth COME - and Spirit heareth what Spirit sayeth ---

So let it profit them which have ears to hear - "Come" - and they shall understand - for understanding precedes the School of Meichezedek ---

One understands the Law - then he does that which the Law requires of him -- Then he is given a part - and a work to do - and it is for the good of all that he is given such a part -- And for his preparation and understanding is he prepared to go forth as one prepared to assist his fellow man -- He goes about in silence preparing himself - and he is not given unto flattery - neither is he given unto flowery speech -- He is aware of that which goes on about him - and he gives no offence - neither does he take offence---

He is of the mind to give as he is wont to receive -- He wearies not of well doing - he tarries not in the places of darkness -- He speaks no evil of his fellow beings - he judges not the heart of his fellow men -- He assists where necessary and expedient - yet he <u>forches</u> not his will upon another - for he is aware of the <u>sanctity</u> <u>of</u> <u>man's</u> <u>free</u> <u>will</u> ---

He grovels not unto man - he asks not of man his opinion - for he knows the fallacy of man's opinions -- He seeks out his own kind - and gives unto him as is needful and expedient - thereby giving assistance unto the Assembly of the Initiated -- Therefore I say unto thee - be ye aware of the needs of thine brothers - that his burdens be lifted - that he might be comforted - and lifted up -- Yet I say unto thee - let not thine own foot drag - carry well thing own load - and be it light.

I am come that it might be --

I AM Sananda

Recorded by Sister Thedra

Beauty
Thanksgiving

This Day is the Day of The Lord -- This is THE Day for which thou hast waited -- This is the day at hand - and the day in which thou hast to do that which hast been given unto thee to do -- No other day dost thou have - save "THIS DAY" - the present day ---

Let thine hand be swift to do Mine Work -- Thine tongue shall be swift to proclaim Mine Words ---

Mine Word shall be thine Shield and thine Buckler - and ye shall stand upon the ROCK which I AM ---

Ye shall not fail - for in Me thou art staid -- Let there be great joy within thine heart this day -- See that which is given unto thee - for this is it given that the Lands bring forth the manifestation of beauty - Peace and gladness -- Be ye blest - for this is the beauty given - and it is for thine own glorification that ye receive it unto thineself -- <u>Bless</u> thineself by the beauty of the Land -- And by the Grace of Our Father is there BEAUTY -- Use it not for self-gratification --

Let it be a time of praise and thanksgiving - for this is it given unto thee -- Let it increase by thine own love and gratitude -- I am One which knows the joy of gratitude - and for this do I praise The Father Solen Aum Solen - for all the Beauty made manifest - all the LOVE gone forth from HIM which is made manifest in the Earth -- Yet I say unto thee - the Earth knows no such Beauty as thine eyes <u>shall</u> behold - for they shall be <u>made</u> to see the GLORY of THE LORD -- For this have I said: "See the Hand of God Move! Behold! See! Know ye that it moveth!"---

I AM Sananda

Recorded by Sister Thedra of The Emerald Cross

Love
Give Ye with Wisdom

Beloved Ones -- Let Us speak of Love -- Love is the Source of all physical manifestation -- Love is the Source of that which is unmanifest and it is the beginning and the end -- While it is the unseen - it is also the seen - for it is that which is unmanifest and manifest - the beauty which ye see - the Cause of the beauty - and that which beholds the beauty is both the manifestation of the "LOVE"of which I speak ---

While the love of man is not even an "out-picturing" or a "poor counterfeit" part of Our Love - or the LOVE is its first denomination - I say it is the lesser - the love man has for each other is the <u>lesser</u> - much less!! - and it is selfish - it is self-love - love of self - which prompts him to give his fellowmen the bitter cup -- For to love one another is to give thine ALL for him - to go the last mile with him - to lay down thine life for him if needs be---

Yet there is a time of giving in <u>wisdom</u> - a time of withdrawal - and a time of waiting - that HE might <u>learn</u> <u>well</u> his lesson -- This is the Word I would give unto thee this day - "<u>Give</u> <u>ye</u> <u>with</u> <u>Wisdom</u>" - and let not thine eyes deceive thee -- It is come when ye shall comprehend that which I say -- Be ye wise in thine giving of thineself - for there are ones which would ride thine back - and then put their foot in thine mouth - See ye the wisdom of silence - where silence is so indicated -- Let not thine tongue betray thee unto the enemy.

I say be ye swift to say that which I put into thine mouth - yet keep thine silence before the enemy -- Know ye him!! - for he shall show his hand!!

This I have declared unto thee - for it <u>IS</u> <u>SO</u> ---

I AM Sananda

Recorded by Sister Thedra of The Emerald Cross

Admonition unto The Candidate

Behold ye the way of The Lord - for I The Lord thy God hast a plan for thee -- A plan do I now hold within Mine hand - I see and know the plan - And by - and thru "THE PLAN" which I hold do I know that which shall be done - for IT shall not fail -"IT" shall <u>not</u> fail!---

For I the Lord thy God hast been sent - holding <u>that</u> Plan ever before ME - that I might bring it before thee ---

I say unto thee: "Be ye as one with IT - for thou art part - and no small part dost thou have"-- So be it that I am He which hast given unto thee the Law - and I have set before thee - the way in which ye shall go and ye shall obey the Law - and prepare thineself for the "GREATER PART" -- For there are things which thou hast not dreamed of - which shall be given unto thee to do -- While I say ye shall do a great and mighty work - it shall be according to the plan -- Yet I say unto thee:

"Be ye as one with IT"- for there are none sufficient unto themself - None sufficient unto themself - NONE so sad as the one which betrays his trust - None so foolish as the one which Thinks himself wise ---

So be it I speak unto the ones which have a mind to follow ME -- For this have I given unto thee the LAW - that ye might go where I go Be ye as ones prepared - So be it ---

I AM

Sananda

Recorded by Sister Thedra of The Emerald Cross

The School of Melchezedek
The Plan / The Harvest

The School of Melchezedek hast been established upon solid ground - upon the Earth hast it taken root -- It IS established - and I say unto thee it shall put out roots into far places - and it shall be as none other - for "The School of Melchezedek" shall be liken unto no other School upon the Earth! ---

For it shall have its roots within the ROCK Which I AM - and it shall not give any quarter - neither shall it take any quarter - it shall be self-contained - sufficient within itself -- It shall go not out seeking affiliation with any other - it shall be as the self-contained School that it is ---

It shall bring forth great and glorious fruit - for it is now time to bring out the fruit which hast lain dormant -- It is the time to bring forth the harvesters - for the season is upon Us -- It is the end time - and the harvesters shall be as ones prepared to go forth to gather in the harvest Let it suffice that I have said unto thee - "the time is come to bring forth that which hast lain dormant". I shall speak unto thee again of the end time - the harvest - the Plan -- So be it I shall lead the ye and I shall give unto thee in abundance and to spare---

I AM Sananda

In Spirit: School of Revelation: this morning --

I Thedra - was working with and in the most beautiful fertile soil - I found so many lily bulbs - I was overjoyed at the find/ by the find - I was transplanting - or bringing them up where they could get the light,

Recorded by Sister Thedra of The Emerald Cross

Upon This Rock I Have Founded

Upon this Rock I have founded the Temple of Sananda and Sanat Kumara -- Upon <u>THIS</u> ROCK I have founded The School of Melchezedek - Which "IS" and hast been before the world wast formed.

I have given unto thee the Laws - the precepts - the power and authority to speak out that others might know - that others might be lifted up -- But none other hast I given the part which I have given unto thee -- Yet others shall have a part - yet unlike thine - for it is given unto thee to be the Priestess of The Order of Melchezedek - after the

Order of thine calling-- And I - the Lord thy God hast called thee out - and set thee apart by the laying on of Mine hand -- I have pronounced the benediction by the laying on of hands - and I have revealed unto thee Mine New Name - and likewise given unto thee thine new name - And the Name of The Father - "Solen Aum Solen" have I revealed unto thee thru thine calling ---

Thou hast heard thine <u>call</u> and answered it - thou hast proven thineself in all ways -- And I say unto thee - thou hast qualified for the next part - which shall be opened up unto thee -- It shall be as an open book - and at no time shall it be closed unto thee - for it shall not again be sealed before thee.

I say - never again shall it be sealed before thee ---

Now ye shall release this Mine Word unto thee - that others might know that which I have said unto thee -- Yet they shall not pilfer these "Mine Words"- neither shall they make a mockery of them - for I say unto them: THESE MINE WORDS ARE HOLY - of THE FIRST MAGNITUDE - and are NOT to be taken lightly by the ones which would but betray themself -- I say - be ye not so foolish - for I am come that this be done ---

Hear ye with ears that hear - for I have spoken that they be heard - So let it be as The Father hast WILLED IT -- Hear ye! Hear ye! and be ye as ones responsible for thine ownself ---

I AM Sananda

Recorded by Sister Thedra of The Emerald Cross

Laborers in the Field

Beloved Ones -- While it is yet time - I speak unto thee of <u>haste</u> -- Haste is that which is meant by continuance - with diligence - and with surety with the mind staid on thine goal - wavering not - departing not from the way I set before thee -- I say - go ye about the business of thine preparation with diligence and patience - knowing that thine feet are firmly planted upon the ROCK Which I AM - and no man shall trip thee up -- Seek only the LIGHT - let thine own Light shine that I might see it - be ye blest that I have found it -- Keep thine lamp trimmed and burning - and ye shall be fortuned Greater Light --

Let it be said that diligence is the forerunner of thine achievement the reward won -- So be it that thine reward is won - thru and by diligence - and application of the LAW -- Let it be said that the LAW is exacting - and none escape it -- While it is given unto thee to be laborers in the field - ye shall reap the harvest - it is said: It shall be Great indeed -- Be ye as ones prepared to go forth to gather - for it is now time of gathering in -- The harvest cometh at its season/ in its season -- There is a time of gathering - too - a time of reaping - let it be a profitable harvest -- I speak that ye might know that which is the LAW -- Heed ye Mine Words - and be ye joyful that this day is come.

I the Lord thy God hast spoken --

I AM Sananda

Recorded by Sister Thedra of The Emerald Cross

It is Not Yet Revealed unto All Men

Beloved Ones -- Mine Word I have spoken - and it is plainly written - that all which seeketh the Light shall find - it shall not be hidden - for it shall be revealed unto him ---

Now let it be written that which I say unto thee -- It is given unto Me to be The Lord God - sent of Mine Father that HIS WILL be done on Earth as it is in heaven -- Now it shall be given unto thee to KNOW the Will of MINE FATHER -- While it is not yet revealed unto all men that which I have spoken unto thee - it is spoken for the good of all men "ALL MEN" All mankind! --

And it is given unto Me to know that which I speak - for I am not given unto idle talk - and I am not of a mind to mislead them -- Be thou this day as ones prepared to follow where I lead thee - and I shall lead thee aright - I shall <u>not</u> mislead thee!.Now let this be recorded that all men might know that which I say unto thee <u>this day</u> ---

It is the fortune which is given unto Me of Mine Father to be HIS SON - a Son of the Father am I - and I am given over unto HIS WILL And HE WILLS that I come unto thee as one prepared - to give unto thee this part which HE hast prepared for thee -- He hast kept this part for thee for <u>this day</u> ---

Now it is come when thou hast sought the Light - and when thou hast surrendered up thine own will - and ye shall be as a fit vessel to receive this part/ "Portion" -- It is for this purpose that I have called thee out from amongst the mass - and commissioned thee to do Mine Work - It is for <u>this</u> that I have set Mine "Seal" upon thee - and no man shall call on thee to do a greater work - for I am commissioned by Mine Father to commission thee for this part of Mine Work ---

Now ye shall return unto the altar which I have set up - and ye shall be given a part - and it shall be given out unto them as it is given unto thee ---

Beloved Ones - the Mighty Cosmos bows before the LIGHT which IS - has always been - and shall ever BE -- Therefore I say unto thee - be ye as ones prepared for the fullness of thine joy - the fullness which no man of flesh can know - for the flesh is weak - and comprehendeth little of joy - the joy which supercedes anything known unto man -- For man is but the dependent of the Father Which is The Fullness - and The "ALL" -- The Father hast brot Us forth from out HIMSELF - that we might glorify HIM - and at no time hast HE denied HIS own Children.

Yet He claimeth not the Sons of Perdition - HE claimeth them not for He hast not created them - they are not His -- They are the Sons of Lucifer - therefore they are not of The Father - they are not capable of ETERNAL Life - they neither have Eternal Life - or the part which is endowed unto thee - as SONS OF GOD -- I say it is SO and I KNOW for I AM of The First Generation - The Firstborn - and I know whereof I speak ---

So be it I AM The Lord thy God -

Sananda

Recorded by Sister Thedra of The Emerald Cross

The Rod & The Staff

Be ye as one which hast Mine hand upon thee -- And ye shall write that which I say unto thee - and ye shall give it unto them as I give it unto thee - for I shall give it correctly - and it shall be received correctly -- So shall it profit them which takes it unto themself - as the Holy Word of The Lord thy God ---

For I AM HE - Which is sent this day - that the WILL of The Father be made manifest upon the Earth -- Now it shall be given unto thee to do the Will of The Father - even as I - for I have given unto thee the Rod and the Staff - the Rod of Power -- I have prepared thee for this part - and it is given unto thee thru obedience unto the Law - for thou hast been obedient - and no place have I found thee wanting ---

Now let this be recorded as I give it unto thee- there shall be no embellishments - nothing added or taken away - for I am sufficient unto Mine own part -- Be ye as one on whose shoulders I have placed Mine Mantle - and I shall direct thee in all that ye do -- So be it I am the Director of this Temple - and I am the One prepared for this day -- Yet I say I bring with Me a Host which are prepared to minister unto thine needs ---

Wherein is it said: that - I know that which is needed for that which is to be done? It is so - So shall it be well with thee ---

I say unto them which hast a mind to learn: First take up Mine cross and follow Me - and I shall lead thee gently -- I say unto thee - I promise thee no miracles - no magic - for I am the Son of God - and I do not satisfy thine own curiosity - I come that ye be brot out of bondage - that ye might be delivered up - that ye might return unto The Father from whence thou went forth -- Let thine eye be single - divide not thineself be ye of a single mind -- Let the Words which I give unto thee become thine - poll-parrot them not - make no mockery of Mine Words - for I am not to be mocked! ---

I say unto thee - be ye as one proven - tried as by fire - and ye shall prove thineself trust worth - and I shall give unto thee that which is kept for thee - for I know thee and thine efforts - which I see and know the motives prompting each one ---

It is said: I come not to give unto thee flowery sermons - and learned discourses -- It is the day of which is written - the day of atonement - judgement - and I ask of thee: Hast thou been found "Trust worth" - hast thou prepared thyself for to drink of Mine Cup?---

I ask of thee: Hast thou prepared thyself to receive Me - hast thou brot unto the Throne of Grace - thineself as a living sacrifice? Hast thou lain aside all thine pettiness - all thine hatred - all thine dogmas - creeds and preconceived ideas of Me ---

I say unto thee: "Cut away thine LEGIRONS - COME FOLLOW YE ME" - and I shall lead thee into the place of Mine abode ---

I go not into the 'dragons den' - I ask of thee obedience unto the Law -- I ask of thee nothing - save obedience unto the Law ---

Allow no man to give unto thee the dregs of his cup - for it is but his own offal - refuse it for thine own sake -- Ask of The Father LIGHT and it shall not be denied thee ---

While I say unto thee - the Light shall not be denied thee - I say take off the dark glass and see it - behold the LIGHT -- I AM the LIGHT - LIFE - and TRUTH --

I AM Sananda

Recorded by Sister Thedra of The Emerald Cross

Sanat Kumara on: "Loyalty"

Beloved of Mine Being -- Again I speak unto thee of "Loyalty" - loyalty unto oneself - and the Source of thine Being ---

For this is the first and last duty of man - for he hast been entrusted with that which is of all things most precious ---

He hast been given free will - and he hast not used it (for the most part) for his own welfare -- He hast sought the things of Earth - and called them 'precious'- yet he hast not remembered that he hast forfeited a Kings inheritance -- A princely fortune hast he forfeited! ---

Now it is come when he shall be given as he hast willed -- He shall be the custodian of his own sowing and reaping - for he hast sown in fields afar - both tares and wheat -- He hast gone in and out of the foreign fields in his forgetfulness - and in his wanderings -- Unknowingly he hast taken unto himself the cloak of Satan - he hast served him diligently -- Yet without the greater knowledge of that which he hast done - he hast given over into this satanic force his will and he hast betrayed himself -- He hast betrayed his trust - for he hast given away his birthright - for a fools penny -- Now he cries as one lost.

He cries as one which hast his neck beneath the tyrants heel - he cries as one trapt - and is he not? ---

NOW it is come when he shall be given as he hast willed - he shall be given por for por -- Four by four - he shall gather in his sowings - he shall be the keeper of his harvest - and no man shall take from him one ounce - one iota of his reapings -- For this is HIS! - and he alone shall judge his labors - for he alone shall count the loss or the gain ---

I say he alone - shall be the judge - for he shall see all that he hast garnered in - and he shall call it good or bad as he sees it - and he shall see it as it is! ---

So be it I speak of necessity - for the time is come when man shall be called forth to face himself - and he shall account for himself - let it be a good accounting -- For this do I say - turn - turn from thine own willful way - and seek ye the LIGHT -- May it be well with thee ---

I AM Sanat Kumara

Recorded by Sister Thedra of The Emerald Cross

The Blind

Beloved of Mine Being -- This shall be given unto them which are of a mind to receive it - unto all which ask for it - the Word shall not be denied them which doth ask ---

Be ye as one prepared to receive it - and ye shall be blest -- While it is given freely unto thee - ye shall give it unto them freely -- So be it that I am the One sent to give unto thee this part - and it shall be for the good of all - so let it be ---

I am come that they be prepared for that which shall come upon them -- It is written that there shall be great tribulations - and it is so - So shall it be --

Yet I say unto them - come ye out from the multitudes - and be ye as one separate from them -- For it is said that each one is accountable only unto himself - for himself - and none other -- While it is given unto each to have a certain responsibility unto himself - unto all others he first must make himself responsible to do that which he should do - he shall first make of himself a responsible person - and for this is it said - 'first unto thine own self be true' for no man can lead aright any man or child - until he hast first cleansed and purified himself ---

For it is by thine own sight - that ye see to lead the blind - yet it is as tho the blind leads the blind ---

I say unto thee: Turn unto the LIGHT - and behold the LIGHT -- And first ye shall be healed of thine own blindness - and then ye shall see that ye might lead thine brother which seeth not ---

No man which is blind hast the wisdom to lead his brother which is also blind ---

Be ye as one prepared - for this is it given unto the physician to prepare himself - that he might heal thru his knowledge of the art which he hast mastered ---

When thou hast been given the cloak of Authority - and the Seal of approval hast been placed upon thee - then ye shall go forth with the authority and assurance that is thine Divine right -- Ye shall bear the Seal or acceptance - and no man shall deprive thee of thine right - for thou hast earned it by Divine right ---

When thou hast prepared thineself to give unto "them" the water of Life - it shall be given unto thee-- Yet no man shall pilfer the Cup - or misuse it - for it is given unto thee in LOVE and wisdom - So be it that I have spoken wisely and with great wisdom -- Let no man take from or add to - for I am the Most Worthy Grand Master within the Inner Temple ---

Recorded by Sister Thedra

Each Unto His Own Part

Be ye as one which I have given this part - this part which is fashioned for thee - it is for thee - and none other - for it shall be for thine own self -- Pass it not unto another - until thou hast drunken of the fullness of its sweetness --

THIS DAY - Let it be said that all which partaketh of the fullness of this MINE WORD - shall be brot out of bondage - let it be ---

For this do I give unto thee this WORD -- While it is given unto them to be within flesh - they shall see with mortal eye - yet when they arise from the mortal fleah - they shall see with the eye of Spirit - and they shall know the Spirit - and they shall comprehend what the Spirit sayeth -- Let it be as they prepare themself - for I am speaking unto them which have set their sails EASTWARD - so let them comprehend that which Spirit sayeth ---

For so long as they but see with mortal eye - they do not see that which is of Spirit -- I say: Oh Mortal - put off the mortal - see with Spirit - see that which shall be, see that which <u>is</u> - and it shall be unto thee an open book -- Let all secrets be revealed unto thee ---

While it is said: "There is no mystery other that thy <u>un</u>knowing-" it is so ---

Yet Spirit shall reveal all things unto thee - when ye have so prepared thineself - be it so - so be it ---

I AM Sananda

Recorded by Sister Thedra of The Emerald Cross

The Will is the Motivating Force

Sori Sori -- Beloved Ones -- The hand is but the hand - while the head is the head - the "Source" the Will -- The hand the instrument - and the action is but that which is willed -- While the Will is the motivating force of "the hand" - it is given unto the hand to obey the WILL -- "The Will is the motivating force" -- So let thy will be THE WILL OF THE FATHER ---

While it is come that great sorrow shall befall the people of all lands I say unto thee - stand ye steadfast - and wonder not at the sorrow - for it is the fulfilling of the Law - let it be - for it is foretold of old that it shall be ---

And at this time I say unto thee - be ye as ones prepared that ye might give succor unto them that sorrow - for sorrow there shall be - let it be ---

Ye shall do that which I give unto thee to do - and ye shall be Mine hand and Mine foot -- Let this be Mine Word unto thee this day -- For this have I spoken ---

I AM Sananda

Recorded by Sister Thedra of The Emerald Cross

Unto the Tried and Worthy

Beloved -- It is Mine time -- Let it be said that this is Mine time - but for that matter thine time is Mine time -- While thou hast surrendered up thine self as a living sacrifice that the Father's will be done in thee – I say it shall be done - and great shall be thine work - as none other -- And for this is it said that GREAT shall be thine part -- So be it that I know that which is to be accomplished - and it is for this that I have extended unto thee Mine hand -- For this hast thou accepted it in the Name of the Father - Son and Holy Ghost -- So be it that I am He which is Sent that ye be lifted up -

So let it be --

I Am Sananda

Recorded by Sister Thedra of The Emerald Cross

God's Mercy

Sori Sori -- Hast not the Lord God spoken unto thee in His mercy and with great love? -- Hast He not given unto thee with great joy - and is it not within the law? Hast He denied thee aught - yea even unto thine lessons?

I say unto thee the way of the Lord is justice and mercy -- Nothing shall be unto thee too much to bear - for it shall be for thine own sake that it is portioned out to thee ---

Let it be said: that they which are of a mind to follow Me shall be tried as by fire - for none follow after Me which are fearful - which are slothful - which are weak of character -- None follow after Me which are of the darkness - for they know Me not ---

Yet when they ask of Me I deny them not - for it is given unto them to have that which they are able to receive - that which they have prepared themself for to receive -- I say they have the capacity - I have the food -- They which have the mind to follow Me shall increase their capacity - and they shall be filled -- Such is Mine love for them - I shall not deny them ---

Let it be said that I know their capacity - their strength and their weakness ---

Call unto the Father that thine capacity be increased - and He shall send One unto thee ---

Let it be for the good of all --

I AM Sananda

Recorded by Sister Thedra of The Emerald Cross

The Banquet

Beloved Children -- The time is come when many shall cry out for assistance - and it is given unto Me to know wherein they are -- And I say unto thee - they are in a pitiful state - for they know not that they forfeit a princely inheritance ---

I say they dine on the husks from the swine's belly - while Mine banquet is spread before them -- I say they know not the delight of Mine banquet - they have not tasted of it - for they think themself prepared for the great feast??

I say they wash their hands and clean their cup before they enter into Mine chamber - that they partake of Mine supper -- For none enter in without first cleansing themself -- They drag not their offal after them - for the stench I abhor -- I say there is no stench about Mine table I am not the porter of their brothels -- I am the Lord thy God - so be it I am not deceived by their trappings ---

I am watchful and merciful and I await their surrender unto Mine call - "Awaken and Come" - and as they are prepared so shall they receive ---

I AM Sananda

Recorded by Sister Thedra of The Emerald Cross

Unto the Opinionated / The Poor in Spirit

Be ye as ones responsible for thineself - ask no favors of any man - forge not thine legirons -- Let thine own light so shine that all might see it -- Feign not wisdom -- Fortune nought unto thineself which thou wouldst not want - for it is now come when ye shall bring forth that which ye have sent out - that which thou hast sown ye shall reap - this is that day - the day of reaping ---

Let it be said that no greater love hast any man than the one which gives of himself that others might live --I say that this is the day when great sacrifice shall be asked of thee -- Ask not for the pleasure of Earth the will of men - man's "Good will" -- Fortune unto thineself the eternal verities - that which shall profit thee ---

Bear ye in mind that all are given as they are prepared to receive -- None are exempt from the law - and unto this I bear witness -- Let not the opinions of man turn thee aside - for I say unto thee - man's opinions are the fetters which bind them/ the legirons which hold them fast ---

Be ye as one which has the mind to follow where I lead thee - and I shall lead thee aright – I speak unto the opinionated and the poor in spirit ---

Lift up thine eyes and rejoice - for it is now come when I shall speak out and ye shall profit to heed that which I say -- So be it I shall speak for the good of all - for I AM

The Lord thy God

Recorded by Sister Thedra of The Emerald Cross

The Way of Man vs The Way of the Lord

Sori Sori -- Let this Mine Word go forth that all might know that I have spoken unto thee Mine servant -- Hold ye the lamp which I give unto thee - let not the flame be touched by the foul breezes which doth blow and which doth fan the lesser flames -- I say unto thee stand firm - for it is come when the frail shall weaken and fall - and these shall find themself insufficient/ unprepared ---

These shall cry out for strength and they shall hear no voice to comfort them - for they have sought comfort in the flesh - and flesh shall no longer comfort them - it shall be as the sting of death upon them -- They shall pray that it pass from them - yet it shall not pass for a time - and it shall be unto them great weight as the lead in the shoe - wherein they shall find themself insufficient - for they have not <u>heard</u> Mine Words - they have not heeded Mine sayings they have not been mindful of them - for they have put things of flesh first ---

They have provided sumptuously for their own comfort - while they suffer their fellows to be given the bitter cup - and at no time shall they escape the law -- Behold the way of the Lord is made strait - I say unto thee make ye haste to do the will of The Father which hast sent Me -- So be it I am come that Justice be established upon the Earth - and that My people be set free ---

So let it be

I AM Sananda

Recorded by Sister Thedra of The Emerald Cross

The Preparation

Beloved -- It is for this that I spoke unto thee in the days of thine misery in the days of thine confusion - when thou didst cry out for light - I say when thou didst cry out for light ---

I spoke unto thee in language strange unto thee - yet therein wast wisdom - for no man knoweth that which wast said unto thee in that day - for it wast the beginning of thine work -- Thy preparation wast great - yet it wast fortuned unto thee to know not that which wast to be it wast not unto thine imaging - for it wast unto thee strange and for that matter great to bear ---

Yet for Mine sake wast thou ridiculed and persecuted - I say for Mine sake wast thou persecuted and or ridiculed So be it I forget not them which I have sealed - and I place not Mine Seal upon the unjust - for I am a Just One - I know the just from the unjust -- I am for that matter not to be mocked -- Many shall go forth claiming to be sent of Me - and they shall be revealed to be false - so let it be --

It is said that in the last day many shall make false claims and many shall be deceived by them -- Yet I say unto them - seek ye first the Light and it shall not be hidden from thee -- Fear not for I am thine Shield and thine Buckler -- Be ye as on which hast the will to know and I shall send One unto thee ---

So be it I am The Lord thy God

Sananda

Recorded by Sister Thedra of The Emerald Cross

On Peace

Beloved Ones;- This day let it be said that it is now come when there shall be wide-spread rumors of Peace; and there shall be <u>no</u> <u>peace,</u> for the peace which they ask is but appeasement. They have not found Peace, for it is not within them - it hast <u>not</u> been established <u>within</u> them. Yet they speak of <u>others</u> as though <u>they</u> had the power to give it or take it away.

I say: "Let Peace be established within thee, and no man can take it from thee". So be it I have spoken of Peace, yet they have not found peace. I have Peace, yet they have not accepted that which I offer them, for they sit in the seat of the scorner - the bigot - the hypocrite, and they speak of Me and about Me, knowing Me <u>not</u>!

I say: They deny Mine sayings; they but mumble that which is accredited unto Me. Yet I say THIS DAY, that they shall hear that which I say, for I shall SHOUT it from the Mountain tops!

I say; "First seek ye the Light, and no man shall close it out".

I say: No man shall deny thee. Let it be: "As thou prepare thyself, thou shall receive", so be it. I say;- "Seek ye the Light, and let Peace be established within thee, and no man shall take it from thee"- So be it.

I AM Sananda

Recorded by Sister Thedra of the Emerald Cross

The Way for Peace

While it is not yet come that they have found Peace, let it be said that peace only comes from within - no man finds it from without, for it is his own inheritance, and he pilfers not that of another.

I say: When they hold subject another, or impose upon another that which they have fortuned unto themself, they shall pay, for the law is clearly stated: "Ye shall not trespass upon the will of another". That implies any body of people; that implies the Countries - the Nations - and the single individuals.

Now, when a plan is established that each one has his own will granted unto him, he shall be solely responsible for the way in which he goes. Each country - nation, or individual,- each shall take upon itself/ himself, the responsibility for <u>its</u> being - or that which hast been brot into being.

While the nations of the Earth are battling for supremacy; I say, none are sufficient unto themself. Let it be understood that the time draws nigh when the way in which the greatest of all Nations has chosen to go shall be cut off - it shall be closed, and their progress shall cease; for it is not given unto the Light Forces to be still - without movement. They move with precision, knowing in which direction they go. Let it be said that aggression shall cease, and it shall not be tolerated! For this hast the Great Assembly raised its Voice. Let it be said, that the <u>hostilities</u> <u>shall</u> <u>CEASE</u>! for this have I spoken out.

Yet there shall be great conflict ere it cease. Let it be, for this is the clearing away for Peace. I say, "They shall learn to <u>love</u> <u>one</u> <u>another</u>, and have Peace within them."

They shall learn from their suffering - so be it the law that they <u>learn</u>! so be it We shall not deny them that. When it is come that they have <u>learned</u>, WE shall then give unto them a hand, and it shall be for the GOOD OF ALL - So let it be.

I AM the One Sent that there be Peace

Light and Love established within them.

So be it I AM

One of the Council

Recorded by Sister Thedra of the Emerald Cross

STRENGTH

Beloved of Mine Being;- Let this be written for them which will that they might read, that they might know that which I say. While they have not the ears to hear that which I say, let it be written that they might read, that they might have the knowledge that there is a "PLAN", and that they are not the creators of it. I say, they run hither and yon, asking of man and his opinion, that they might find consolation in their own.

And it is for this that I speak out at this time. When it is given unto man to know his Source, he shall at no time ask of another 'his opinion', for he shall have the knowledge of all things what-so-ever - he shall no longer ask of others his opinion about anything, for he shall KNOW - and for a surety!

I say: When he hast become unbound, he shall know! and be as one wise!

Yet it is given unto man as a whole to seek for Light, and he knows not whither to go that he might find it. He hast neither the mind nor the will to search out the Light; to seek out the Light that he finds his way. I say, it is given unto them to weary of the search; they falter near the attainment; they heed not the admonition: "COME". I say, they weary and fall by the way.

Hear ye that which I say, and know ye that there are many prepared to assist, yet they have their hands above thine head; They are not thine servants; They give unto thee work which shall be done, and at no time shall it be more than ye can bear. They give generously of themself that ye be strengthened in thine weak parts, and that ye be about the Father's business.

So be it that I am one which hast given of Mineself that ye be spared this day that ye be as ones prepared, that ye be kept for this day. Now it is given unto Me to know that which lies before thee, and I speak wisely and with compassion.

Let it be written, that the time draws nigh when the floods shall rage; the fires shall take many forms, and it shall lay waste the wonderlands of the world. It shall leave behind it the blackness of destruction and desolation; it shall sweep the lands wherein there is great and marvelous forests; it shall be as ye have <u>not seen</u>!

Let it be written that: the water shall be of no avail, for the waters shall not be unto them comfort; it too shall be as one gone mad; it too shall be as ye have not known, for the lakes shall dry; the rivers shall change their course - they shall overflow their banks; the dams shall break. And I say unto thee: They shall be as ones entrapt, distraught, and there shall be great loss of property, and many shall lose their forms of flesh.

Now for this have We said: "Prepare thineself". Fear YE NOT! and seek no hiding place, for there is no hiding place, I say; "Seek ye the Light", let Peace fill thine heart, and know ye that ye are NOT alone.

So be it I am One which stands by to give assistance - be ye as ones prepared to receive it, for it is proffered in Love and Mercy, and with Wisdom. Be ye blest of Mine Presence.

I AM thine older Brother and thine Sibor,

Sanat Kumara

Recorded by Sister Thedra of the Emerald Cross

The Holy Words Shall Be Brought to Pass

Beloved Ones; - Hear ye this, and know ye that this is the Day for which thou hast waited. Let it be said that <u>this</u> is the DAY of the LORD, wherein all the Prophecies shall be fulfilled - wherein all the Holy Words shall be brot to pass. I say, this is the "Day of full-fill-ment" and for this hast thou waited; for this have We, the Mighty Council waited yet not in vain.

I say unto thee: The Sacred Writ shall be remembered, and it shall be brot to remembrance in the days of fulfillment - for there shall be cause for remembrance. And when it is come that they are brot face to face with their foolishness, they shall be reminded of their folly, and the Words which have been given unto them, that they might have WISDOM.

I say; It hast been repeated many times: "Look ye unto the Father for thine sustenance, and know ye that He is the Giver of Life - He is the cause of thine Being". And He gives and He takes without revenge. So be it that He hast given unto thee graciously and lovingly, and then I see them turn their face from Him and seek in dark places for wisdom!

Wherein have they found their freedom? surely not in the world of men!! Wherein have they found Peace? Surely not within the "World of Men"!

I say: I come not to <u>bring</u> peace; yet I come that they might know from whence cometh their peace. Let it be established within them, and no man can then take it from them.

So be it I have repeated it many times, yet there is <u>no peace</u> within them which cry Peace! Peace! Peace! They but make a mockery of the "WORD", and at no time shall they find it without - they shall establish it within themself, then they shall be as ones prepared for the "Greater Part". Let it be.

I AM Sananda

Recorded by Sister Thedra of the Emerald Cross

Ye Walk Not Alone

Sanat Kumara speaking:- With the Love and Compassion which is Mine, I bow before the Light which I serve, and I place within thine hand Mine hand, that ye might take it - that ye might have Mine assistance, that ye might know that ye walk not alone.

So be it that I am One of the Mighty Council, and at no time shall WE betray Our trust - neither shall We forget that which hast been said unto thee.

Let it be said this day, that the Way is opened for thine return unto thine abiding place. I say, ye shall return unto thine Source and receive thine Inheritance in full. Now let it be said; <u>Not all</u> shall accept the Gift of comprehension; not all shall accept the Gift which has been given for their acceptance,- they have but to prepare themself for to receive it.

It is said: "Cut away thine legirons, ye cannot bring them into this place", for therein is wisdom.

When it is said: "Prepare thine self" it is little understood by man! for to prepare thineself is to be able to receive the <u>Greater</u> <u>Part</u>; and it is the law: The "Cup" shall first be emptied out - cleansed, that it be filled with the <u>First</u> <u>Substance</u>, that of Light Substance, which is the first and pure Substance. <u>This</u> <u>is</u> <u>the</u> <u>turning</u> <u>away</u> from the old - the putting on the NEW; the shedding of the old garment - the taking up the new, the bright and shining Armor of God. The Light is not tarnished, it is pure, shining and dazzling to behold!!

I say unto thee: Place thine hand in Mine; accept that which We offer unto thee, and be ye as one free forever - <u>for</u> <u>this</u> have I revealed Mineself unto thee.

Blest are they which know me, for I am He which is known as Sanat Kumara

Recorded by Sister Thedra of the Emerald Cross

Sori Sori -- Be ye as one blest this day - and receive ye him which is come that ye be blest of him - for this one shall be unto thee all that the Father would have him be -- At the first let it be understood that he comes with the consent of the Father - The Mighty Council - and by thine own consent shall he speak unto thee of the things which are to be done -- So be it and Selah -- Be ye as one prepared to receive him - and let it profit thee --

The Master in General

Be ye as one which I place mine hand upon - and ye shall be blest of me and by me - for I come with the consent of the Father and The Mighty Council -- Hast it not been said that I shall speak of that which is to be done?

Now it shall be given unto us to go into the secret places of the Most High - and be unto the children of the Earth a "Grand Master"- The Master in General - for the school of Melchezedek shall bring forth a teacher which shall be <u>strong</u> and which shall not fail -- He shall walk among men of the Earth as one of them - and he shall be as one prepared for he cometh at this time for to lift up men - which hast lost their way I say he <u>has</u> come that men shall be lifted up - that they be brot out of bondage---

Now for the first time I say unto thee: Thou art as one which hast been prepared for this day -- Be ye as one on whose head I place mine hand - and I so speak unto thee that ye might know that which hast been foretold -- Ye shall be as one which hast been ordained and prepared thru the ordination - to take upon thyself such responsibilities as follow such ordination -- Be ye as one prepared to give as ye have received - for this do we say - be ye as one prepared -- For that are ye now prepared - that <u>all</u> men might come into their Sonship ---

The door now stands, ajar - and there is room within the Inner Temple - and there is yet time -- It is said: "Come" "Come ye hither and partake of the Life which is free unto all"-- Yet none enter into the Holy of Holies unprepared -- Hasten ye and enter herein - for herein ye shall find thine inheritance which hast not been spent ---

For this day let it be said - that the Council hast sent forth one which shall walk the hiways - the biways - with humble heart and heavy feet which shall tire of the way - yet he shall be as the one sent - and he shall not fail - he shall call forth the power and force which shall be his to command -- He shall be unto <u>man</u> a shining example and for this shall they see his light and follow him -- He shall walk with surety and patience - knowing that which he is to do ---

Forever shall ye remember that which I say unto thee - for he shall remind thee of these mine words -- It now behooves me to say: Ye shall know him for that which he is - for he shall make himself known - and ye shall be blest to know him -- Let it be as the Father hast willed it -- I am he which is come to remind thee - for this am I sent -- Be it so that I am he which shall stand by thee in the Inner Temple and hear the words "Well done my good and faithful servant"- be ye as one blest this day -- I am

The One to Come

Sori Sori -- Be ye as one prepared to give unto them as I give unto thee for in so doing ye shall bless thyself - for this do I say - bless thyself -- Now it is come when one shall go out from the place wherein ye are -

and he shall be as one prepared to give unto others - for he shall have mine hand upon him ---

He shall stand before the Great and Mighty Council and find himself proven worthy -- He shall find himself approved of by the Council - and he shall give of himself that others find their way -- So be it that I have spoken - and it shall be as I have spoken - so let it be -- At no time shall I be unto mine own self untrue neither shall I mislead thee -- It is said that one shall be sent - and it is so - and no man shall set foot against him - neither shall he bow down unto any <u>man</u> - for he shall do honor unto the Father which hast sent him - for from the throne of God - <u>the</u> <u>Father</u> he cometh - I say - from the throne of God he cometh -- So be ye as one prepared to receive him for he has the authority and the power invested within him of the Mighty Council - and he shall be true unto his trust -- For this is he sent - that the Father's will be done -- So be it and Selah -- Come ye forth and partake of mine blessings - and give thanks unto thy <u>Source</u> of <u>Being</u> - and praise the Father Solen Aum Solen for His Grace and Mercy -- Let thy heart sing praises unto Him - for He <u>is</u> the Source of thy Being ---

Let this day bear fruit - and let it be the day of remembrance -- So be it and Selah

Recorded by Sister Thedra

A Revelation

This vision was given me a couple of hours before the foregoing communication: -

The scene opens on the side of a mountain - very steep (The High Holy Mountain) - - The light broke thru the darkness on the scene - soft like moonlight thru the tall pines - - I sensed the pine needles making a soft deep cushion - very slippery - - there came into my vision a team of 120 animals - headed strait up the side of the mountain -- I thought: what a strange combination - six animals abreast - 20 in length - the outside row on each side were horses - the next row mules - the center 2 rows bulls ---

First - I could see only the feet straining! slipping on the needles! getting no place - yet with such great effort! - each animal pulled in its own way - at its own tempo - with its own strength - not in harmony with the others - - simply could not harmonize - their natures being so different! - lots of power - yet unto destruction - because of the combination! - - Then in the subdued light falling only on the scene I saw the animals were wearing great heavy harness - much iron on them - - so heavy I thought ---

Then came into view the wagon to which they were hitched - - it too was heavy like an ore truck - - then I beheld some men on it - - At this point the animals lost their footing - somersaulted backward - wagon and all - spilling the men down the hill I sent forth a decree (prayer) that they be not crushed by the wagon or team - - I saw them spill - roll - tumble free - - some lay as if dead - unconscious - some rolled down into the deep blackness below -- (above the scene was a dense fog - or pre-dawn light)

I noticed the clothing of these men - that of prisoners - - I commanded that the only one who was able to get to his feet be brot to me - - he came and stood before me - - I noticed his weary body - sweat and humility ---

This is pertaining to the world conditions this day -- Give it some thought ---

War makes strange bedfellows - - None take the High Holy Mountain by brute force - - their instruments (wagon) shall be overturned - - None ride the band-wagon to glory - the summit - under such a strange team -- Man shall be saved - yet he shall come in humility and sweat - his salvation shall be earned - he alone must pull his own weight - it is a single file up "THE PATH" (ref. the Scripts of Sananda) - "THE PATH OF INITIATION IS STREWN WITH THE BONES OF THE ONES WHICH DID NOT MAKE IT"

"Let Peace be established within YOU - sayeth the Lord of Hosts.

Sister Thedra of the Emerald Cross

The Crown of The Son

Sori Sori - Hear ye me this day - and give unto them this mine word - which is given unto them which seek the Light -- I say unto them: "Behold ye the way set before thee - behold the Light - walk ye in the Light"- suffer not thy foot to slip - keep ye the way - and fret not for them which rebel against me - for I am that I AM - and I change not for their rebellion -- I am changeless - I go not - neither do I come - I am ever present -- I fear not their rebellion - scorn - neither do I put my hand against them -- They set their hand against me - for this do they put themself out - for this do they war - for this do they the things which are not of me -- And for this do I send mine servants into the "world of scorn" that they might know the way - find it and keep it open - and walk in the way that leads unto <u>Mine</u> <u>House</u> ---

Now ye shall counsel them as I have counseled thee and they shall heed that which ye say unto them - as ye have headed mine counsel -- Forget not that I am thy Father Eternal - the Source of thy Being! I am He which is ever present - ever near - nearer than thy hand or thine foot for thine hand and thine foot are mine - in me - of me - and by mine own body hast it been brot forth into the world of flesh - flesh made seen - and for this have I said - let it be ---

So be it by mine own hand do I now speak unto them which do have a mind to learn - let them learn of the Father and me - the beginning and the end -- For this have I sent thee forth into the realm of flesh as mine servant - as mine own hand made flesh -- Speak mine words - and let them hear - and know -- While they fall on deaf ears they are not void for they are words of Life! Light! and shall not perish ---

So be it I shall put mine words into thy mouth - and it shall profit them to listen -- As they receive mine words - so do they receive me - and I shall touch them and quicken them - and they shall be raised up and they shall have peace profound - and they shall not want -- So be it and Selah ---

Hold ye steadfast and falter not - for I am He which abideth with thee - thou in me - and there is no separation - for all <u>is</u> One -- And this is mine word - for I am - and thou art one in me - not divided - not separate - yet one there be - forever - yea forever -- Hold high thy head walk ye which way thy Crown tilts not -- Blest are they which receives his enua -- Be ye as one on whose head rests the Crown of the Son of God ---

Let this be Mine Word unto thee this day

Recorded by Sister Thedra

From Out the Cosmos

Sori Sori -- Now is the time for reflection - and it is given unto thee to be as one which hast mine hand upon thee - and I say unto thee: Be ye as one blest - and for this shall ye rejoice -- I speak unto thee from out the Cosmos - the place wherein all things are known - wherein there is no mystery -- I say herein is no mystery - for this is mine place - and none shall say me nay - I know - and I am the one which hast given unto thee thine gift - and none shall take from thee that which I have given unto thee -- For this do I say - be ye as one prepared for the greater part -- Be ye as one watchful - and know ye that I am with thee - yet ye shall walk the way I point - and ye shall not fail ---

Blest are they which follow where I lead - for this do I say "Follow Me" -- Wherein is it said - I shall lead thee into the place wherein there is peace profound -- So be it and Beleis - let it be

Ask of the Father

Sori Sori -- Let this day bear fruit -- Be ye as one alert and give unto them this mine word - for it shall profit them - and they shall be as ones responsible for that which they do with these mine words ---

Bless thyself to receive them - for it shall profit thee ---

When it is come that they are discomforted - they cry out for help - yet I ask: What hast thou contributed to the comfort of the host? What hast thou contributed unto the whole of mankind? Hast thou given of thyself?

I ask of thee that thou mayest know thyself worthy of the assistance of the ones which have gone before thee - ones which have given of themself that the Kingdom of God be established upon the Earth ---

Let not them which sit within the dark chambers and ask of the dead put upon thy head more than thou canst bear - for I say - they would but hold thee bound -- Let it be said that the <u>Great</u> and <u>Mighty</u> <u>Council</u> is fortuned that ye be free -- Ask not of another - ask of the Father - the Source of thy Being - for in Him art thou staid -- So be it and Selah ---

While it is yet time I say - pick up thy feet and walk ye erect - head high -- Put away thine pride and come as ones humble of heart - and ask of the Father - and He shall sustain thee -- Fortune unto thyself Peace - let it be established within thee and no man shall deprive thee thy freedom - for no man can give or take from thee one iota of that which thou art -- Art thou at "Peace"? Art thou at Peace? Art thou peaceful? Do ye know where peace is to be found?

I say - Peace is to be found in thy <u>Oneness</u> with He which hast sent thee forth as all living being - for from His own word hast thou come forth as His hand and foot made flesh -- So be it and Selah ---

Hold ye forever unto the Light and falter not -- Wait upon no man harken unto mine words - praise ye Solen Aum Solen - Source of thy Being - for in Him thou hast thy Being - for that art thou here - for this have I spoken that ye be reminded of thy Source -- So be it I am one with HIM - and I know myself to be - Let freedom ring - let it peal out for all - yet ye shall not falter - neither shall ye fear -- Bless thyself to KNOW from whence cometh thy freedom - look unto no man - for no man can stay the hand of the One - Father - Solen Aum Solen - for He is the Source - the Source of all good and glorious gifts - and He shall endow the righteous with the Gift of Peace -- So be it and Selah --

Recorded by Sister Thedra

The One Who Comes with Authority

Sori Sori -- For this day let it be said that one shall come unto thee - and he shall have upon his head the Crown of the Sun - he shall wear well his crown - for he shall be true unto his trust - he shall be as one qualified to give unto thee that which he has for thee -- So be it ye shall receive of him - and give unto others as to ye have received -- So be it, it shall profit thee --

Be ye as one on whose head I place mine hand - and ye shall be blest to receive of me -- And they which receive of thee shall be blest in like manner -- I say ye shall bless them in like manner -- So let it be that they which seek the Light shall receive these mine words and be blest thereby ---

Now it is come when one shall go forth as one which hast been sent: He shall be one which hast been chosen for his part - he shall be the one which hast come at this appointed hour - for the work at hand -- He shall do that which he came to do - for he shall not fail! - for he knows well that he is sent - that he has the authority given unto him of the Father - thru the Mighty Council - and for this is he now come ----

For this do I say unto thee - keep thy eyes open - fear not - walk ye upright - and see ye that which is now being brot forth - even in these days of trial and temptations - I say it is the day of awakening! -- Lo it is come when men walk the hiways and biways with fear and trembling yet for this have they prepared themself - for they have fed the dragon he hast fattened on the blood of the innocent - he hast been fed well -- Now he shall die of his own gluttony - he shall be as one rendered helpless - for he shall find no feeding place -- He shall lie helpless and die of his own overfeeding - his own over gluttony ---

Be ye as one prepared to take from him the dainty morsels which he loves so well - and he shall be deprived of his substance - and of his appetite -- Let it be said that he - the dragon - lies in wait that he might consume the nations of the Earth - yea - even the Earth and all its peoples! -- I say unto the Nations of the Earth: Empty out thine house of all profanity - hypocrisy - all blasphemy - all that which is not of the Father - and be ye aware of HIM - and in HIS NAME do ye these things Be ye as ones prepared to go forth in the New Day as ones made new - Let the word go forth: "This is the New Day - when all things shall be made new"---

Faint not - neither look ye back and lament for the fallen - nor neither shall thy tears or words atone for them - they have served the time - and the day of their serving shall be remembered as the days of darkness ---

Now remember ye this is the dawn of the New Day - which shall be the "Age of Light" - yet there are ones such as do well in the valley of despair - which shall not see the Light - the Sunrise of the New Day they have not heard the trumpet sound - the Call of the <u>New Dawn</u> - they are looking within the dark crevices wherein lurk the vermin of mankind -- I say - look ye upward - from whence cometh thy help - rest ye in the knowing - <u>help cometh</u>! Help is now come - KNOW ye it is come!

Be ye blest to know - - let it serve thee well - for this is it sent --

I am one sent -- Hold ye high the banner of TRUTH and JUSTICE abide in the LIGHT - and I shall give unto thee in great measure --

Recorded by Sister Thedra

99 & One

Sori Sori -- Now it is the time that ye bring forth that which I have kept for this time -- Ye shall give it unto them which are prepared to receive it - and it shall profit them to receive it - even as it shall profit thee to give it ---

Now for this day let it be known that there are none which are unaccounted for - none overlooked - for each is named and numbered for I say unto thee - the parable of the 99 and one - is not a parable only it is the part of the Father's Wisdom and Plan that all be accounted for I say each is numbered and named -- Remember - it is said: "Not a hair on thy head falleth unnoticed" "Not a sparrow falleth unaccounted for"- - I tell thee all things are accounted for - all things are according unto a law - and that law is accurate and exact ---

Put not thy trust in the arm of flesh - place thy hand in mine - and I shall lead thee - I shall put mine hand out and ye shall take it in trust and faith -- So be it that I shall direct thee and lead thee - that ye do mine work in joint with me - in connection with me and the host -- The Mighty Council shall be as thy servants and as thy Sibors -- So be it and Selah ---

Walk ye as one sober - fear not - stand ye tall - and fear not the mockery hurled at thee, for I say - it is but the foolishness of them which know not -- Rest in me - the One which knows the LAW of thy BEING and I shall pour out upon thee the Water of Life - and ye shall be as one made new- as one made whole -- So be it and Selah ---

Play thy part well and ye shall come into the part which is kept for thee -- Hear ye that which is said unto thee and it shall be given unto thee in greater measure - let it be --

Recorded by Sister Thedra

Thy Cup Shall Overflow!!

Sori Sori Be ye as one prepared to receive that which I bring unto thee for it is expedient that I give unto thee this portion - and it shall be given unto them which await it -- It shall bless them and they shall know that they have been blest to receive it -- Wherein is it said that we watch that which they do with the word which is given unto them - - and unto them we say: Be ye blest -- And as they receive - so shall they be blest according unto their capacity to receive -- So be it the law ---

Portion out thy own time and effort - that we might come in and speak unto thee - that we might commune - one with the other ---

Now I say unto thee - ye shall prepare the ground for the seed - and after the seed comes the harvest ---

Therein is the joy of waiting - let not thy cup run dry - for there are ones which would give unto thee that it be filled to overflow -- Let it be - to the brim - to the overflow - that they drink of the overflow - - this shall be sufficient unto the thirsty! - for I say - thy cup shall overflow!!

So be it that I am he which knows thy capacity - and it shall come to pass that thy capacity shall increase - and thy strength shall be sufficient unto thy increase ---

While it is now come that ye shall be fraught with distractions - I say unto thee - give not of thy time unto them which are but curious - and would but belittle thy efforts -- Count them as but the poor ground which is yet not fertile -- So be it they shall be given the "Word" as it is prepared and it shall suffice them -- Let them read as they run - let them prepare themself -- And fear not - for I see and know them which are prone to speak that which is not prompted by love - they see not that which is hidden from the eyes of the unjust -- So be it that I am he which stands upon the High Holy Mount as One which Knows --

So be it and Selah --

Recorded by Sister Thedra

Let it Be Understood

Sori Sori -- Let it be understood that the way is now open before thee - and it is clear -- And it shall be given unto me to keep the Way of the Lord - for I am He which is Sent that it be kept open -- Now I say: "Come ye which will - come ye which are of a mind to enter in - into mine Father's abode" ---

Rest in the knowing that He hast a place for thee - wherein ye shall abide in peace - and wherein there is no division - - <u>One</u> in Him - and of Him brot forth ---

Let it be understood that He hast sent thee forth - and by His Grace shall ye be brot back ---

For this do I come that it be so - so <u>let</u> it <u>BE</u>!

I am that I AM

Recorded by Sister Thedra

God's Word

Sori Sori -- Let it be understood - there is but One Lord God - of Earth for which the Earth is held upon her course - her foundation -- And as for that I am the One which is responsible for her course and for her position -- Yet there are many which have their part - yet they are as ones which have the part allotted unto them - such as keeping watch -- And their stations are various - and they are as ONE in manner - and as one man they man their respective offices - and direct as with one mind one purpose -- So be it that there is no diversity of purpose in them ---

They know their part well - and there is no mis-judgement or misunderstanding - for they are well trained -- So be it that I have called thee out from them - and set thee apart that ye might be the director - the head of this <u>Mine</u> <u>Office</u> that I have allotted unto thee - by the authority invested in me -- Now I say unto thee - the time is come when ye shall stand on such authority as I have invested with thee - as by the initiation thru which thou hast proven thyself - thru which thou hast qualified and proven thyself trustworthy ---

Now - ye shall stand upon a solid foundation and declare thyself - and know ye that I am with thee unto the end -- So be it and Selah

Recorded by Sister Thedra

Phantoms of the Night

Sori Sori -- Say unto them - that there is but one Source of their <u>being</u> and that is Solen Aum Solen -- So be it and Selah -- Now ye shall give unto them the WORD as thou hast received it - for it is pure - undefiled and it shall remain uncontaminated - worlds without end -- So be it and Selah---

Hear ye me - all ye children of Earth! Consider well thy part - and fear not for thy life - for it is indestructible - it is of the Father - given unto thee as of Him - and by His own Will hast it been given -- No man shall fear - for his fears are but phantoms of the night - which shall pass in the light of day ---

I say - behold ye the Light! Arise from thy slumbers - and be ye as one come alive - - Wait not for another - for I speak unto thee - unto each and every one which slumbers ---

I say - slumber no more - ARISE! come forth as one alive - walk ye with surety - for I have gone before thee to prepare the way -- Before it is too late - let it be said - I have done my part - and I am not yet finished -- I am not finished for I await thy coming - and it shall be a glad day when ye come unto me - for all the Host shall sing <u>together</u> one glad anthem of joy: "Hail! Hail the Sons of God!"---

Let it be - for this are we gathered this day - let it be a glad day ---

Hear ye me - all ye that have ears to hear - all ye that have eyes to see -- See the hand of God move - for this am I sent --

Recorded by Sister Thedra

Sheep - Goats - Wolves & The Good Shepherd

Sori Sori -- For this day let it be said that there is but One Father - Source of our BEING - and in Him we have <u>our</u> "Being"-- So be it and Selah ---

Adore Him! and keep within thy heart the flame - and the <u>portion</u> which He has allotted unto thee - for He is the ALL in ONE - in <u>Him</u> all IS - <u>All</u> is in Him -- And that which is real and eternal is of Him - and He is the ONE in which all reality has its being -- So be it a truth - and a reality - that I am that thou art - and we are ONE in HIM ---

Now I come unto thee that we might be of service unto them which know not -- I say unto thee: There is work to be done within the place wherein ye are -- And it behooves thee to be as one alert - and know the sheep from the goats - the sheep which are fortuned the mind to learn - the ones which are prepared to learn. Deny them not yet ye shall stand tall - and with feet firm. Ye shall not allow them which have their hands fast beneath them* come unto thee empty of hand and put their hand into thy pocket - and then speak idly of thee - and thy household.

I say - thy house is the "House of the Lord" - Keep it holy -- Be ye watchful - and keep watch over the sheep which hast the mind to learn contribute not unto their slothfulness - for it is unbecoming of the "sheep" which have entered into the fold of the "Good Shepherd' -- I say: The good shepherd knows his sheep from the goats - - likewise he is like unto the Father of his children - He is mindful that the wolves lurk about in dark places - laying in wait for the unprepared -- I say - be ye as one prepared to prepare them - as thou hast been prepared -- Yet - they shall first be mindful of thy authority - and from whence it comes --

Hold thyself in readiness for the part which shall be given unto thee for it shall be as none other - and no man shall deny thee aught - for I say unto thee: Ye shall walk and not weary - ye shall run and not faint for the Almighty Hand of the Host of Hosts shall give unto thee as thou needst -- So be it and Selah ---

Let it be as the Father hast willed it - - So shall it be -- I have spoken by the authority invested in me thru the Council of the Great and Mighty Host (The Council of Councils) for there is none Greater! ---

So be it I am but one which hast a part - none smaller - none larger, for all parts are as necessary unto the Great Whole - the great and perfect plan -- So be it we have the Greater Vision - for this we say: "Be ye alert! and come forth as one prepared for the greater part"---

For this do we stand by that we may give assistance when needed - So be it our part to assist - for this have I come -- Praise ye the name Solen Aum Solen - for this hast the <u>name</u> been revealed unto thee - years past - for it is He - that holds us all within His Radiance - within His hand we move and have our being -- So be it and Selah---

None shall turn thee aside - none shall put their hand unto thy mouth. So be it thy voice shall be heard thruout the land -- Hear ye me and I shall speak again - for the upliftment of mankind shall I speak --

Recorded by Sister Thedra

Responsibility

Sori Sori -- Let it suffice thee that there is but One Lord God -- Yet there are many which come unto thee which have His hand in theirs - which come by the consent of the Council -- And each and every one contributes their part - and they bless thee by their part - and none are denied their blessing which receive them --

I say - they come that all be blest - for theirs is a selfless service - and they are alert - for this hast been their work for long - and they know their part well -- They have been found trustworthy and responsible - so be it they shall not deceive thee or lead thee far afield.

They shall be as ones responsible unto themself for that which they do for they know the law - and the responsibility to be great!

Bless them with thy attention and obedience - thy respect and devotion ---

I tell thee of a surety - they are mine own - and I have brot them forth that this work be done with great efficiency - for I tell thee - that there is great purpose in that which we are doing herein -- Let it be understood that there are many which would come in to deceive - and to destroy that which hast been brot forth - but I have established mine guards wherein they hold forth - and wherein they hold fast the Light that ye stumble not - wherein ye might be safe - and wherein ye might walk knowingly --

Now I speak unto them which have sought such guidance - that when they have been found trustworthy - and when they have become sufficiently prepared - I shall give unto them that which is needful - so be it in keeping with the law - for I know mine rights - mine authority and I am within the law when I give of mineself - mine own gifts - and of mine time - for I judge them not -- I see and know that which they are prepared to do and to receive - so be it lawful to give according unto their preparation ---

Wherein have I failed them? They are responsible for their own preparation -- Have I not prepared mine own self for this part? ---

What greater service could one perform than to reach a helping hand unto them which cry for assistance - that they be brot out of bondage -- So be it mine assistance I extend to all - yet they are prone to reject me - therefore mine assistance - therefore they wait ---

Be ye as one ready to receive my blessing/ mine assistance -- For this do I say unto thee: I am Come! for this have I revealed unto thee first the Holy - Blessed Name of Solen Aum Solen - that the men of Earth might come to know and rejoice therein -- And I say - blest shall they be to <u>know</u> that name - and they shall use it wisely -- Poor in spirit is he which profanes it - or desecrates it - for from the Father Solen Aum Solen have they their BEING -- So be it and Selah ---

Holy - Holy - Holy is the name Solen Aum Solen --

Recorded by Sister Thedra

Spirit Ministery

Sori Sori -- Hast it not been said that: "One shall come unto thee"- and hast he not been sent? I say - he is come - and for this is he prepared to give thee assistance -- Ye shall now be as one prepared to go into the places wherein thy assistance is needed - and ye shall minister unto them as is necessary - that they may be blest of thee - as ye have been blest of Him -- So be it and Selah ---

Wherein is it said - that: "As ye are prepared so shall ye receive".

Now ye shall have the assistance of the Mighty Host - and they shall be unto thee all that ye shall have need of - - for this have we said: "Prepare thyself - and we shall do our part" ---

Let this day bring forth fruit - and it shall be sweet indeed and in truth ---

While it is said that ye shall go into the places wherein ye shall minister unto them which are prepared to receive thee - I say - ye shall be unto them as thy Sibors are unto thee -- Ye shall minister unto them in spirit and in truth -- So let it be - for it is for the good of all that we come unto thee - - that ye be as one prepared to lift them up -- Praise ye the name of Solen Aum Solen -- Hear ye that which He says unto thee - and it shall be well with thee -- So be it and Selah ---

Wherein hast it been said that ye have been called out from them which serve self - and wherein they sit in the places of darkness that "self" be gratified -- Now I say unto thee: "Yield not thy ground - stand ye firm - give no ground - and be ye steadfast"---

Let it be said that there is a legion to sustain thee in thy appointed task which I assign unto thee - by the authority which has been - and is invested within me of mine Father which hast sent me ---

Now ye shall be as one blameless - and shameless - for ye shall stand with me unashamed and blameless - for I have given unto thee the name - Thedra - which is not of Earth - which is transcendent - which is of realms yet unknown unto thee -- I have first revealed unto thee the name - Sananda - which is the name which ye know me by -- which all initiates this day shall come to know me by -- I have given unto thee the Father's name - which shall be known thruout the Earth - and I say: "Unto Him every knee shall bow - and every tongue shall sing His praise"-- So be it and Selah ---

Let thy feet be swift to do His Will - thy heart filled with joy - and thy way shall be illumined by the Light of the Christ - which goes before thee - that ye fail not ---

Blest be the feet that are swift upon His mission -- Blest be the surety of purpose - blest be the word of Him which shall be put into thy mouth -- Blest thy hand - for it shall be as balm unto the heavy of heart and succor unto them which mourn -- So be it I have come at this early hour when they sleep - and when thy hands are at my service and command ---

Now it is given unto me to say unto thee: "Walk ye tall - walk ye with circumspection - walk ye which way thy Crown tilts not for have I not ordained thee my priestess - mine prophet"-- Know ye that I am aware of all thy needs - and I am not a pauper - neither do I grovel unto any man -- I say - I grovel not - for I am sufficient unto mine own self - therefore I provide for mine own household - I give unto them as is expedient - and needful ---

Therefore - I say unto thee: Be ye as one prepared to go forth as a soldier of the Cross - the Cross and the Crown shall be upon the banner which shall go before thee - and this shall be thy Shield and thy Stay - Thy banner shall be mine banner - and thy hand shall be mine hand - thy foot mine foot - and ye shall run and not be weary - and ye shall know no sorrow ---

So be it I have touched thee - and thou hast been alert and found me to be at thy side when asked -- Fear not that I forsake thee -- Let it be said now - that I have appointed thee mine prophet - - Mine hand I place upon thy head in holy benediction - and I say unto thee: Ye shall give this mine word unto them which have prepared themselves for to receive it - and they shall be blest to receive it - for it shall carry with it great blessings and strength - for these are mine words - and no man shall deny them - - neither shall any man set his hand unto mine mouth - for I shall speak that which I will - and it shall be for the good of all mankind -- So let it be as the Father hast willed it I am come that He - be glorified -- So be it and Selah ---

Hail! Hail! Hail! unto thee my Beloved!

I say unto thee: Hail! Hail! Hail -- For blest art thou - blest shall they be which do receive of thee --

Recorded by Sister Thedra

The Order of Business

Sori Sori -- Let this be recorded as I speak - for it shall be given unto them as it is given unto thee - in words which they can comprehend - and none shall say me nay -- For I am come that they might know - that they might have such knowledge as I am prepared to reveal unto them.

It is said - first they shall receive mine servants - the word which I give unto them - then they shall accept me - receive me - for <u>then</u> shall I reveal mineself unto them which receive mine servants - which bring unto them mine word ---

Now ye shall say unto them: "In the name of mine Father I speak unto thee" - for I have given unto thee the gift of communion - the gift of communication with the realms of Light - with the place wherein the Father abides ---

I say: Ye are one chosen - for thy preparation hast been long and plentiful - complete - and rewarding -- So be it and Selah ---

Now ye shall hold high the banner of the Christ - which shall be as thy banner - for it shall go before as thy shield - for it shall be known in the time which is at hand as the banner of Truth and Justice -- It shall be as the banner of the New Day - the New Dispensation - the day when I come to call forth mine own - the ones which shall accept me for that which I am - the Son of God -- And likewise they shall come to know me as Sananda the Lord God - Sent of Him which is the Giver of Life. Life of His Life - the Fountainhead of All Life ---

Now ye have established thyself - and found me as one reliable - for wherein have I failed thee? I say - ye shall be as I - true unto thyself unto thy trust - and I shall lead thee into fields afar - yet ever nearer - near- and yet nearer - and ye shall stand with me upon mine High Holy Mount - and ye shall be as one blest of me and by me - for this have I given my word -- I have said: "Ye shall prepare thyself and I shall do mine part"-- I have said: "Prove me and I shall not fail thee" - and mine word hast been proven true -- Mine hand hast led thee and blest thee in ways unknown unto then which are yet in darkness ---

I say: I am the one which laid the Corner Stone of this Temple - this house -- I set up the house in the name of the Father which hast sent us forth to Glorify Him - that His Will be done - that His Kingdom be established upon the Earth ---

I have set thee apart for thy service - for thy loyalty - and for thy love of righteousness - and I have given unto thee that which thou hast done without flinching - - and ye have given credit where credit is due Thou hast been obedient in all things - and now ye shall walk knowingly - and speak on thy own behalf -- For this I have ordained thee as "Prophet/ Priestess"- as the one set apart - and over mine sheep.

I have called thee the "Good Shepherdess of mine flock - which I shall give into thy keeping ---

For I shall give into thy keeping part of mine flock - and ye shall tend them as the "Good Shepherdess" - for ye shall tend them with dignity and with love -- Ye shall know them - and they shall come with humility and great haste -- Ye shall know them - for I shall place mine own mark upon them - and they shall know mine words which I shall put into thy mouth -- They shall accept thee and mine word - then I shall reveal mineself unto them - for I shall remove their blindness when they are so prepared -- At last I speak unto thee as thou hast prepared thyself for to receive -- So let it suffice at this hour - 4:40 AM So let it be that ye shall be blest this day - and be ye as the hand of me made manifest - and give unto them the blessing which thou hast received of me -- So let it suffice them - for the day is sufficient unto their needs - and as <u>they</u> are prepared - so shall they receive ---

Now ye shall go into the place wherein ye shall receive instruction which shall give unto thee greater knowledge - greater strength and wisdom - that ye might lead mine flock into greener pastures - into greater vistas - broader horizons wherein they might be prepared for the greater part -- Let it be as the Father wills it - - for this hast He sent thee forth - that He be glorified in the Earth as He is in Heaven ---

There is a prayer which says: "Thy Kingdom come - Thy Will Be Done on Earth - as it is in Heaven" - so let it be - and be ye as His Will let His Will be done in thee - thru thee - by thee - and for thee - - for this have I sibored thee --

Recorded by Sister Thedra

Lead On

Sori Sori -- Praise ye the name of Solen Aum Solen - and prepare thyself for thy new part -- Let thy heart rejoice that this day is come - for it shall be a glad day ---

Wherein hast it been said that the time swiftly comes when one shall stand upon mine High Holy Mount - and see that which is in the world of men - and that which torments him shall be revealed unto him - and that which is of the Light shall be revealed - yet fuller and in greater measure -- So be it and Selah ---

Fortune thineself to be one which is given greater capacity for knowledge - and ye shall stand tall and know for a surety thou art prepared for that matter which is now shown unto thee ---

Let us proceed into yon heights with greater swiftness - greater caution - and greater wisdom - for the time is precarious - and the way is filled with pitfalls -- So be it that I shall lead thee gently and ye shall not fail - neither shall ye falter -- Bear ye in mind that I am come that ye be lifted up - that ye be unbound - and for that do I say - be ye of sure foot -- Let it suffice - that I lead thee - and ye shall be as one able to go where I lead thee -- Fear not! - Waste not thy energy on them which would turn thee aside -- Let thy hand be mine - and forget not that I am with thee -- So be it and Selah ---

Fortune thyself the part which shall be new and strange unto thee - and ye shall not fail - neither shall ye want - for I am thy provider - and I am thy fortune - - give unto me credit for knowing thy needs-- So be it that I am he which hast called thee forth - now ye shall stand with me and mine strength shall be as thy strength - for mine shield and my banner shall cover thee - and ye shall know no despair -- No evil shall befall thee -- So be it and Selah

Recorded by Sister Thedra

Mission Statement

Give the truth to the world. Let it be received where it will. Many will read the messages. Some will accept the truth, others will read through curiosity, a few will ridicule. Yet to all is the truth given, and to all remains the power of choice.

The hope of the world in these times is in spiritualizing all forms of activity---promoting understanding through love and service. These must be the watchwords if the world is to come into lasting peace. We are trying to influence a world that is going astray and could cause undreamed of suffering. We are trying to overcome the thought of materialists and to bring a spiritual outlook into the earthly life. We need the help of all on earth who can think in spiritual terms. The great battle to be fought now is between the spiritual and the material, between idealism and carnalism. You can help by spreading the word---we are asking that you help because the battle may be long and the victory far away.

Halls of Light is not allied with any sect, denomination, political entity, organization, neither endorses nor opposes any cause. There are no dues for membership. Halls of Light is self-supporting through its own voluntary contributions. Halls of Light has but one purpose: to help through encouragement and understanding...

To contact the publishers or to obtain copies of our other books, please contact us at email: goldtown11@gmail.com

Sananda's Appearance

Be ye as one which hast heard Mine Voice and responded unto it - for I speak that ye hear, and I say that which is wise and prudent.

Let it be known that 1, the Lord thy God hast spoken and bear ye witness of Me, for I have made manifest Mineself that ye might know Me - and for this wast these manifestations made.

I say that I have made Mineself manifest that ye might see Me with thine mortal eyes; that ye might bear witness of Me. Yet thine companions saw and believed not; neither did they hear, for they were selfish and unprepared - yet, did I deny them?

I say; I came that they which would might see and hear. I went and came again unto Mine own. So be it that I have found; I have given unto the found that they which know not might know; that they might come to know as thou knowest.

Yet, how many hast turned from Me and persecuted thee for Mine Word. It is said, "Woe unto them which persecute Mine servants." is it not the law which they set into motion?

Yea Mine beloved, I say they bring about their own downfall. So be it that I am a compassionate one, and I would that they know what they do. So be it they shall learn well their lessons. So let it be, for this is the mercy of God, the One which hast sent Me.

So be it. I AM The Wayshower, the Lord thy God

I AM Sanand

About the Late Sister Thedra

Since the later part of the last Century, the Kumara wisdom has begun to reemerge into the world. This process began with the late Sister Thedra, whom Jesus Christ appeared physically to while on her deathbed and spontaneously healed her of cancer while she was in the Yucatan, where she had gone to accept her fate and the will of our Lord Jesus Christ.

That is when something miraculous occurred. Jesus spoke to her saying, "My name is Esu Sananda Kumara" and then sent Thedra down to the Monastery of the Seven Rays in Peru to learn the Kumara wisdom. After five years, Thedra was told to return to the United States where she founded the Association of Sananda and Sanat Kumara at Mt. Shasta in California.

While heading this organization, Thedra channeled many messages from Sananda and taught the Kumara wisdom. He introduced himself to her by his true name, "Sananda Kumara" And it was by his command that Sister Thedra went to Peru but eventually left upon being told that her experience there was complete. She then traveled to Mt. Shasta in California and founded the Association of Sananda and Sanat Kumara. A.S.S.K.

You ask, Is There a difference between Jesus and Sananda? Our Lord's name given at birth by his Father Joseph and his beloved mother Mary was Yeshua, thus being of the house of David and the order of Yoseph, he would be called Yeshua ben Yoseph. The Roman Emperors placed the name of Jesus upon the sir name of Yeshua after the Emperor Justinian adopted Christianity as the official faith of Rome and ordered that the sacred books be compiled upon approval of a specially appointed counsel appointed by the Emperor into a recognizable and uniform work titled "The Bible". Prior to this, there never was a Bible per se.

There existed until the time of the Emperor's edict, a selection of many Sacred texts that were employed in the Sacred Teachings, many of which were copies of what the Greeks had transposed from the original texts in the Libraries of Alexandria which were originally compiled by Alexander the Great, and were destroyed by Julius Caesar, fearing that they might prove dangerous to the rule of a Caesar, an Earthly God.

In addition, it was to keep the knowledge of Alexander's Libraries out of the hands of the Ptolemy's who were said to be descended from his bloodline. At the time, Caesar had no way of knowing that vast portions of the Library were already in the Americas, in the Great Universities of the Inca, and in possession of the Mayans.

Yeshua spent many years in the East after his ascension. The Good Sheppard, upon his appearances to the Apostles after his ascension, told them that he was going to tend to his Father's other sheep; which meant, plainly, that he was continuing upon his sacred journey. As The Ascended One, Yeshua took to himself the name of Sananda, meaning the Christed One, and Sananda was thus embraced forevermore by the Great Solar Brotherhood. To many of you this is all new, to others it will be received as a welcome easing of the wall that has so long separated two sides of the same coin. This is being placed into the ethers and the matrix of thought at this time, as it is the time of The Great Awakening, and the Christos is already emerging into the new consciousness.

Authority to use the name of Sananda was given to Sister Thedra when Jesus, (Sananda), appeared to her in the Yucatan and cured her instantly of the cancer that had taken over her body. Further, he allowed a picture of his countenance to be taken at that time that she might realize the occurrence was more than a dream. Thedra had a large format camera called a 620 that she used to take the picture of Sananda.

Sanada's Message to her by Sister Thedra: "Sori Sori: Mine hand I have placed upon thine head, and I have given unto thee the authority to use Mine name. Give unto them the name Sananda, by which they shall know Me as the Lord thy God - the Son of God, sent that ye be made to know me, the One sent from out The Inner Temple that there be Light in the world of men. Now it is come when ones which have the will to follow Me shall come to know Me by that name which I commanded thee to give unto the world as Mine New name.

There are many that shall call upon the name of Jesus, yet they will deny the new name as they are want to do. Unto thee I give assurance that I am the One sent that there be Light in the world of men. Now let this be understood, that they that deny Mine New Name deny Me by any name. So be it I have appointed thee Mine spokesman; I've given unto thee the power and authority to speak for being that which I AM. And I say unto thee Mine child whom I have called forth and anointed thee with the Holy Spirit, thy name shall be as it is now called, Thedra, that name I spoke unto thee from out the ethers, and thou heard Me and accepted that which I gave unto thee; and wherein have I deceived thee? Wherein have I forgotten thee, or left thee alone?"

I say unto thee: "Mine hand is upon thee and I shall sustain thee and you shall come to know that which I have kept for thee. So be it that I have kept thy reward, and at no time shall it be dissipated or scattered, for it is intact. So let this Mine Word suffice them which question thee - let them question, and I shall bear witness for thee. For do I not know Mine servants from the traitors? Do I not reward Mine servants according unto their works or merits? I speak that they might know that I am mindful of Mine servants, that I am not a poor puny priest who has forgotten his servants.

"I say unto them: Mine servants shall be glorified above the crowned heads of the nations which have set themselves apart, and denied Me Mine part of Mine word for they have turned from Me in their conceit and forgetfulness. Now let this go on record as Mine Word, and I shall give unto them proof, which are of a mind to follow Me. So be it as I have spoken and I am not finished; I shall speak again and again, and I shall rise Mine Voice against them which set foot against Mine servants, and they shall be as ones cast out. So let them ask of Me and I shall enlighten them. So be it I know whereof I speak. Be ye as ones blest to accept Me and know Me for that which I AM." On Saturday, June 13, 1992, at exactly 10.00 PM, at the age of 92, Sister Thedra made her final transition from the comfort of her own bed. When the time arrived, she simply took one small breath and slipped quietly away, without pomp or fanfare.

She left as she had lived: as a humble servant for the greater good. The messages included were given to Sister Thedra shortly before her transition. They are compiled here to give you some idea of the significance of her passing and of the expansion of the work, as she is now free of the physical limitations and the pain of the past. Her work now in the higher realms will simply be an extension of that work.

Divine Explanations

Part - I

The following explanations and definitions of terms used by Sananda (Jesus) and the various Sibors were given by Sananda through direct revelation. They are not alphabetical. These explanations should be read over and over.

- - - - - - - - - - -

"My Beloved Sibors please give us plainly the definitions of the following words that there may be no error on our part." - Thedra.

THEMSELF? What is the explanation of your terminology of "Themself" – "themselves"?

"I (Sananda) say unto thee mine beloved, they which would be unto thee a vessel, unto thee a sibor, unto thee teacher, are as ones enlightened of the Father, enlightened of the Father for the light is in them.

They know their parts well, they have their memory, they have mastered the elements, they can do all the things which I do and they take unto "themself" no credit for they have overcome self. They are self-less. Now I say unto them: them which work with thee are the Selfless ones. They ask nothing for "themself." Now while this is true they are as one.

They are within the great brotherhood of the Selfless Ones - the Ones clothed in white. They are as the Royal Assembly - and each unto his own, yet each for all and all for one. Now while in thy world, they (of thy world) are <u>selfish</u> and they are not for the whole - they ask for self and I speak of these as the selfish ones. I speak unto them in terms which they shall come to know and therein is wisdom.

I say that they shall be responsible for "themself" and as a world of me I say they shall be responsible for their society; they "themself" have created it. Now I speak unto thee mine beloved, I say "ye shall be responsible for thyself. He shall be responsible for himself. They as a whole shall be responsible for that which they have created, while thou art responsible unto thyself for thine part - and not held accountable for theirs. Be it so."

BELEIS? "Mighty is the word and great the power thereof. I say unto thee this word carries with it the part of surrender. The word is the release of power - that which is sent forth by the one which asks of the Father His blessing. It is the surrender of the self - the complete surrender of the personal will and letting the Father's will be accomplished in all things through thee. "<u>So</u> <u>be</u> <u>it</u>" - it the accomplishment, the acceptance of the Father's plan."

SELAH? - "The word carries the Seal of Truth - meaning it is without error - no mistake - it is the verification of Truth - not subject to change.

SIBET? – "The Sibet is one which has offered or presented himself as a candidate for the greater learning and for the greater initiation. He comes as an empty vessel that he may be filled. So be it."

SIBOR? - "I am the Sibor of Sibors." - "The Sibor is one which has been illumined of God the Father. He has returned unto the Father purified. He has gone the Royal Road - which means he has overcome death. He has mastered the lower elements - he controls the elements. He can raise the dead - heal the sick - he can create like unto the Father <u>for</u> he has finished his course and won the victory and returned unto the Father the Victor. So be it."

"I am the Sibor of Sibors. I am the first born of Him which hast sent me. Sananda."

LEGIRONS? - "Beloved - I say unto thee: thy opinions and thy dogmas are not the least of these - neither thy creeds. Be it ever that these are great and heavy ones. Now let it be understood that a leg-iron is something which holds thee bound. It is something which holds thee, it keeps thee fast, wherein progress is not possible. Now that progress be made possible, ye shall cut away the legirons.

Knowest thou these bound by legirons? These are to be pitied, they drag them with them, impeding their progress - and they are as ones bound! They are not free - are they? While they serve their sentence - they are as ones bound - they are bond-men - they are bound men - men bound. Now let me say I too am a "bondsman." I came that they may be free. I say I bring unto thee the law which thou shall obey - unto the letter - then I shall give unto thee that which I have kept for thee. Be ye as one prepared for that.

PREPARATION? Now - preparation - what do you mean by "preparation?" "This my beloved is the part which they shall do - the part of preparation is: cleaning thyself of all the opinions, indoctrinations of man. The cup must be emptied. This is thy part, the becoming the '"little child" unopinionated, unscathed and unmarred with or by their doctrines, creeds and crafts. I say the child is unindoctrinated and un-opinonated and is the virgin mind – (yet it does not remain so long in this world). While the little child represents the empty cup - the empty vessel, the Virgin Spirit, it is given unto the child to be one which has come from other realms and to have been in many embodiments, many times: yet the symbol of virginity. Wherein is it said there are none innocent among thee?

WHEREIN I AM? - "Now while thou art yet within the world of men - I am within mine Father's realm, the place wherein there is no darkness, wherein <u>ALL</u> things are known. I say wherein <u>ALL</u> things are known, wherein there is <u>No</u> mystery.

And too - I say when thou hast attained unto thy Royal Road, when thou hast become part of the Royal Assembly, thou shall know as I - thou shall be as I - thou shall be brought into the place wherein I am, for I say unto thee this is attainment. This is the day of Attainment, the day of "becoming," the day of thy salvation. Know ye that this is Mine day - the day for which thou hast waited? I say unto thee: "This is the day of fulfillment. This is Mine Day. Mine Day is come ---"

What is meant by "ALL THE LANDS OF THE EARTH?"- "This I mean, all the lands of the Earth. I have said it, I mean it as I have said it and there is no mystery of or to it."

ALL MANKIND? "This is Mine people - Mine children - Mine flock - Mine Church - Mine brethren - Mine congregation unto whom I shall minister. By Mine own hand shall they be fed and led. These have I came to find. Are not all <u>hu</u>-man beings considered "Man kind"? by thine own standards. Yet all men are not of me."

WHAT DO YOU MEAN - "WILL IT SO"? - "There is power in the "WILL" and the power which they use to create their own torment and confusion is misused energy. Yet they will this - they will it so. Now when ye will to serve me ye give unto me thy undivided attention, the whole heart - thy heart - thine ALL. Yet I say that they which doth attempt to serve me with one hand and the dragon with the other has not willed to serve me. They are not of me - they are not of Mine flock. I say they are either with me or against me. I cannot accept the one hand while they reserve the other for the dragon. They are not wholeheartedly mine.

I make no compromises with the dragon. Mine shall come out from them and surrender unto me themself - their all - without reservation. This is willing it so - for they will the Father's will be done in them, through them, by them. They leave no energy that the dragon may use. They use all their energy to serve me. This is mine word unto thee."

WHAT IS DARKNESS? - "Thine Un-Knowing - thy darkness comes from the fall of man - which one was with God the Father perfect which didst have his memory blanked from him when he didst transgress."

MAYAS VEIL? - "The result of such unknowing - the darkness which man has brought upon himself. The part he has created for himself."

WHAT DOES IT MEAN TO <u>BETRAY</u> <u>ONES</u> <u>SELF</u>? - "This is the sad part for first the 'fall' came from his betrayal - and it hast resulted in the fall - in the veil of Maya - the "illusion" and in thy un-knowing - in thy own darkness."

WHAT OF BETRAYING "HIS OWN TRUST"? - "The plan is all inclusive and includes <u>all</u> - yet there are ones unaware of the "plan" - (and they are not as included in this temple as yet) - no personal reference unto the ones within this temple. Now when one becomes aware of his part, he is given the law and it is provided for his own good and he has the law clearly stated, plainly recorded, and he turns his face away - that he may hide from it. He puts his fingers into his ears that he may not hear it. He gives unto his benefactors the bitter cup and he goes his own willful way.

He has betrayed himself for he shall be caught up short of his course. When he has been given a chance - a "part" within the plan and he has committed himself, he has the responsibility given unto him for that "part" and should he be so foolish as to betray his trust he shall be like unto one which has thrown overboard his <u>own</u> life belt - poor foolish ones!"

WISDOM? - What is meant by the word "Wisdom?" - "Wisdom is that which is light, the knowledge of the law and its proper use. The right use of the law - and this Mine children is Mine part. I come that ye may BECOME wise! Wisdom is thy divine gift - not of man, for man of Earth is foolish indeed - and he is nothing save that which the Father has endowed him. All else is of the world of "illusion" which shall pass into nothingness in the Light which I Am."

WHAT IS THE "PEARL OF GREAT PRICE, THE PRICELESS PEARL? - "That which I offer thee - thy freedom, thy salvation from bondage - thine inheritance in full - Mine word which is not purchased with coin - not bought, neither is it sold. It is the wisdom of which I speak. Mine offer unto thee is without price - it is the 'pearl' - "Mine Pearl."

WHY ARE MIS-SPELLED AND GRAMMATICAL ERRORS USED IN THESE SCRIPTS? - "I am not a conformist. I am not concerned with the letters of man for I am He which has come that they be unbound by their fetters. I say unto them which desireth the letter - unto them the letter.

I say unto thee: be ye as ones free from such bondage. I stand ready to free thee from thy bondage. Unto thee I say - give unto the letter no thought. <u>Hear</u> what I <u>say</u> for I shall say it in many ways as becomes me and serves mine purpose. I say I am no stranger in thine midst. While they know me not, I know them. I see them bowing down before the Golden Calf - and they worship at the shrines which they have set up. (Their own standards of education.) They guild them and bring unto them burnt offerings - yet they close me out.

Be ye not so foolish. <u>Be ye not so foolish</u>! I am come that ye might have Light - Wisdom - Freedom which is the Father's will. While the letter changeth and passeth away - and the letter is not the law - the letter is of no consequence other than to cause thee to see the "Word." The word is the power which shall provoke thine mind into action and thy mind shall be free from the letter. See what is meant within the Word, and let thine mind be staid on <u>me</u> - the Light, the Way - Truth and Wisdom."

"I am He which hast come - that ye be free: forever free. I am Sananda - Son of God. Once known as the Nazarine, He which was born of Mary, Ward of Joseph.

Recorded by Thedra

Part - 2

THE WHITE BROTHERHOOD AND THE EMERALD CROSS.

THE MANY QUESTIONS ABOUT THE WHITE BROTHERHOOD AND THE ORDER OF THE EMERALD CROSS MAY BE EXPLAINED IN A FEW SIMPLE WORDS.

ONE HAS TO EARN THE RIGHT TO BECOME A MEMBER - EITHER IN THIS LIFE OR OTHERS BEFORE OR AFTER - NONE ENTER UNPREPARED.

THE WHITE BROTHERHOOD - or - THE ROYAL ASSEMBLY is of the Realms of Light---not of Earth. The Ascended Masters have proven themself in the school of Earth (THE SCHOOL FOR GODS) who have trodden the path of INITIATION - overcome the trials and temptations of the mundane world - who have gained their freedom and ascended as the Lord Jesus Christ (Sananda). They have gone the ROYAL ROAD.

Knowing the path of the Initiate -- and its pitfalls -- and sorrow, they extend a hand in Fellowship - LOVE and WISDOM - NEVER depriving the candidate an opportunity to learn his lessons well -- for this is His salvation -- for this do they proffer their hand, NOT to do our part for us, but rather that we become strong and free by our own strength.

The Royal Assembly or the White Brotherhood have known all of the heartaches, the longing, crucifications, temptations and JOYS of the aspirant -- the candidate -- the Master -- the Sibor -- herein lies their strength, their understanding, their great love for us on the path.

Their love and understanding knows no bounds. They give help when necessary for our progress. They also withhold it wisely - should it deprive us of our lessons. The candidate on the path of initiation shall become self-responsible for all his actions -- all the energy allotted him throughout his whole EARTHLY existence - and make atonement for all his misused energy, for therein is his salvation.

There is no one else which will ever make this atonement for us (the candidate) on the path of unfoldment. While the host of "WHITE BROTHERS" Brothers of LIGHT are ready to assist, the candidate shall (MUST) put forth every effort to overcome all the forces of darkness which would deter his progress and earn for himself his freedom from BONDAGE.

THE EMERALD CROSS

THE EMERALD CROSS is a company – and an order of beings who work within the Brotherhood of MAN - and the Fatherhood of God - for the good of all mankind --- And at the head of this group is one known as MOTHER SARAH, the personification of love -- embodiment of all MOTHERS. That is: the LOVE of God made Manifest - in MOTHERS. The blessed Mother Sarah is the head of this Order of the Emerald Cross. And when one earns the Divine right and privileges to associate themselves with this Order, it is the joy of all the Orders - and Brothers of Light. I speak for the Order - for I am known as Merseda. (As told to Sister Thedra of the Order of the Emerald Cross).

COMANCHE - which is the porter at the door - which doth keep out the unworthy, the unjust, the unclean. The Door Keeper - the one responsible for the Temple Gate.

BITTER CUP - that which you would not like to partake of - that which poisons thee, that which is not good, that which torments thee - that which ye have given unto thy brother to torment him which returns unto thee as a boomerang to torment thee - which ye shall receive multiplied - which has accumulated in its swift flight. I say prepare not for thyself the bitter cup for ye shall drink of the portion which thou doth prepare for thy brother. Be ye not foolish - make it not bitter.

BLEST OF MINE BEING - I have given of Mine self that Mine beloved has being.

BLEST OF MINE PRESENCE - Have I not gone the long way? I have gone out from Mine place of abode that I might bring light unto the Earth that she might be lifted up - that the children thereof might be delivered of all bondage - that they might return unto the place from whence they went out. And have I not come unto thee many times that this be accomplished? Have I not done all which has been given unto me to do? Wherein have I failed thee? Have I not done all that I have come to do? - While it is not as yet finished, I shall not fail. My mission shall be finished ere I return unto Mine abiding place. Shall I not be unto the true and shall I not return the Victor?

GAVE OF HIMSELF - Did I not give of Mine Self - hast thou? Have I not been true unto Mine trust? Have I asked aught for Myself? Have I not done that which I have promised? Have I not given Mine All? Have I not come on a Sacrificial Mission? What more have I to give - other than myself?

PORE - The physical body - vehicle which thou dost use.

INITIATION - Thy preparation for the inner temple. Each step is an initiation. One step at a time - the overcoming of self - the world - the becoming that which I am.

COSMOS - That which is unseen throughout many universes by thy eyes. Great is the expanse of the Father's Kingdom and the total thereof is referred to as "throughout the Cosmos."

LORD'S STRANGE ACT - This I shall reveal in Mine own time.

WALK WHICH WAY THY CROWN TILTS NOT - as a Son of God. Do honor unto thy Father Mother God - and thou shall be as one which has the Royal Raiment upon thine shoulders - and ye shall wear it in honor and with dignity.

WHEN IT SAYS IT IS RECORDED - WHEREIN IS IT RECORDED? - In the secret place - in the eth - and within the inner temple - and wherein thou art are many things recorded - which I do speak of. Ye shall see these recordings when thou doth enter into the secret place of Mine abode. I say ye shall read the records wherein are written the records of all thy travels from the time ye left the Father Mother God until thine return unto him.

WHAT IS MICHAEL'S FLAMING SWORD? - "The "Sword of Truth and justice."

Recorded by Sister Thedra

Other Books by TNT Publishing

Who am I and Why Am I here?

The Significance of Existence

Death and the Incredible Life After

Fear of Death Removed

Paradise Regained

Spiritual Laws Revealed

Unseen Forces

Too Good to Be True

The Truth of Life in the Spirit World

He Who Has Ears

The Great Awakening, Volumes I thru VII

The Great Awakening, Volume VIII,
THE WHITE STAR OF THE EAST

The Great Awakening, Volume IX,
I THE LORD GOD SAY UNTO THEM

The Great Awakening, Volume X,
MINE INTERCOM MESSAGES FROM THE REALMS OF LIGHT

The Great Awakening, Volume XI,
THE BOOK OF THE LORD

The Great Awakening, Volume XII thru XV,
TEMPLE TEACHINGS FROM THE HIGHER REALMS

Transfiguration Volumes I thru Volume VIII

Contact us at

Email: goldtown11@gmail.com

Web: https://www.whoamiandwhyamihere.com/

www.ingramcontent.com/pod-product-compliance
Lightning Source LLC
LaVergne TN
LVHW051547070426
835507LV00021B/2448